THE ORIGINS OF KUWAIT

THE ORIGINS OF KUWAIT

by B. J. SLOT

E. J. BRILL
LEIDEN · NEW YORK · KØBENHAVN · KÖLN
1991

With thanks to Dr Sultan bin Muhammad Al-Qasimi, Mr Khaled Al-Duwaisan, Dr S.K. Al-Shuhaiber, Mr Salem Al-Zamanan, and Mr Joop Korswagen.

The paper in this book meets the guidelines for permanence and durability of the Committee on Production Guidelines for Book Longevity of the Council on Library Resources.

ISBN 90 04 09409 1

Printed in The Netherlands

Table of Contents

Introduction

Writing the history of the Gulf States in the seventeenth and eighteenth centuries is much like writing the history of many parts of Europe in early medieval times. Relevant material is scarce, amounting to little more than one or two small references amidst a mass of irrelevant data. Few references to the history of the Arabs of the Gulf are to be found tucked away in the tomes of trade papers of the Dutch East India Company's establishments in the Gulf.

The worst problem facing a historian of the Gulf in the early modern period is the lack of local source material. In the case of Kuwait, there are no old, local documentary sources, and even the investigative zeal of A.M. Abu Hakima could only unearth quite vague and secondary references from eighteenth-century Arab sources. One might contemplate looking into European sources, but there one would find that, in early modern times, the Europeans were concentrating on the two or three main ports of the Gulf and that Kuwait was usually outside their scope. Abu Hakima found most of the few documents and sentences referring to Kuwait's early history in British archives.

A few other sources remain open to research. One way of tackling the problem would be to examine old European maps and nautical charts of the Gulf in order to find out if there have been evolutions in the way in which the area of Kuwait has been depicted. The results of a comparative study examining the European (Portuguese, Dutch, French, Danish, German and English) cartography of the Gulf area since the first features of Kuwaiti territory were noted in 1570 are recorded in this book. Maps are, in some respects, difficult historical sources; the presence of a certain place on a map certainly proves its existence at the time the map was produced, but does not give a date of origin for that location. Nevertheless, it was possible to use maps to clarify Kuwait's history.

The data found in the maps and charts can be linked to certain documents. The Dutch documents contain the oldest references to the existence of Kuwait, but have never before been used to the full. This book is an attempt to forge links between maps, nautical charts, references in contemporary travel books and archival documents.

In the end, we managed to find some material on the period before 1775, thus enabling us to shed more light on this obscure period in the history of Kuwait. After that date, British documents become more plentiful. Our research concentrated on the collection kept by the General State Archives of the Netherlands. We give the texts of all Dutch documents, and many other relevant contemporary European documents on the territory of Kuwait for the period between 1645 and 1775. This book also contains a sample of photographs covering all significant cartographic currents relevant to the area of Kuwait up to 1820, with some later samples up to 1864, the period in which the first really reliable nautical charts of the Gulf appeared.

Part I
ILHA DE AGUADA

There are no known historical documents which refer to events in the territory of what is now called Kuwait.
The area is marked on old maps. The oldest mention on European maps of any part of the territory now forming the present State of Kuwait, is that of Ilha de Aguada for the island Faylaka.

An outline of the history of the Arabian side of the Upper Gulf between c. 1560 and 1660

For a few decades in the sixteenth century, the territory which is now Kuwait was part of the Ottoman Empire. During the second half of the sixteenth century, the Ottoman Empire lost its grip on the coastal areas of the Gulf. Originally, during the rule of Sultan Süleyman the Great (1520–1566), the Ottoman Empire had followed an active policy in the Gulf, consolidating its hold on Al Hasa and attacking the Portuguese and their Arab allies in the area of Bahrain.

The struggle between the Ottomans and the Portuguese took place in the area of Bahrain. At that time, the name Bahrain was used not only for the island, but also for part of Al Hasa and the coastal area of much of the Upper Gulf. However, in the latter part of the sixteenth century, the Portuguese and Ottomans alike became the victims of increasing pressure from a stronger Persia as well as from Arab tribes. The outlying Ottoman territories of Al Hasa and Basra came under serious attack and had to be defended with the help of the Portuguese.[1] Basra became a semi-independent principality, ruled by an Arab family which had acquired hereditary command over its Janissary garrison.

Although the Ottoman Sultan, in all important documents of state, proudly continued to call himself Lord of Basra, Bahrain and Al Hasa, these were largely empty titles. The Provinces of Bahrain and Al Hasa had been reduced to the sole town of Qatif, the remainder of the area was controlled by Arab tribesmen who were in a permanent state of war with the Ottoman Empire. The principal among these tribesmen were the Banu Khalid. The Pasha of Basra followed his own independent policy, only nominally recognizing Ottoman sovereignty. In reality, Basra was a beleaguered fortress. Arab tribesmen controlled most of the area outside the walls of the town.

The territory in which the present State of Kuwait is situated was called in Ottoman legal language the 'Land of the Tribes', the wilderness outside the limits of the 'Well-protected Empire'. Since the beginning of the seventeenth century, no serious attempts had been made by the Ottomans to acquire control over the tribal area. The Ottomans actually lost territory to the tribes when the Banu Khalid acquired Qatif around the year 1660.[2]

This is how the area of Kuwait came to be part of a large desert area where Ottoman armies did not dare to penetrate. The Banu Khalid controlled the area, and Kuwaiti local tradition relates that the early origin of the town of Kuwait was a summer residence of

[1] Cordeiro, *Dois Capitães*, p. 116.

[2] The best source on the loss of Qatif by the Ottomans is Thevenot, *Reizen*, vol. 2, p. 278. Longrigg, *Four Centuries*, p. 113 has a slightly different story, but Thevenot is the most reliable source.

the Shaikh of the Banu Khalid, which was established sometime in the seventeenth century.

In written historical sources before the year 1645, there are no references at all to the area of Kuwait except for the mention of a few names on old maps. These maps are the oldest sources making direct reference to Kuwait.

The earliest maps

Much of the earliest European cartography adds nothing to our knowledge of the area of Kuwait. This school of cartographers originated in Venice and extended to the famous Antwerp cartographer Ortelius and the Amsterdam cartographer Blaeu in the sixteenth and seventeenth centuries.[3] They mostly produced maps with fabulous names attached to geometrically distorted drawings of the coast of the Gulf.[4]

The first known maps to show something real in the area of Kuwait are manuscript maps produced in Portugal. The earliest I could find was a nautical chart by Lazaro Luis of 1563.[5] Portuguese maps give two names in relation to Kuwait: off the coast there is an island called Ilha de Aguada (Island of the Well), and one or two small islands or cliffs, called Dos Porcos (Two Pigs). Some maps give nautical indications near the islands, which is always a sure sign that European shipping has passed through. There can hardly be any doubt that Ilha de Aguada is the island Faylaka, and, as such, these maps are the oldest historical maps containing references to parts of Kuwaiti territory. The reference to Dos Porcos is more difficult to locate, Awha being the most probable choice. Near Awha there is a low rocky patch two feet above the surface, which is almost a small island. This could have been the second of the 'Two Pigs'.

Some Portuguese maps and maps derived from them of a later date contain two other names: Sar, usually on the mainland opposite Ilha de Aguada, and Hadaviza, which some maps also situate on the mainland. It is not really feasible to make identifications of these names. It would seem attractive to connect Sar with places like Ras al Zor or even Jahra, but these are very hazardous guesses. Likewise it is impossible to identify Hadaviza, which continues to figure on more recent maps.

3 This tradition seems to have started with the map *Il desegno della seconda parte dell'Asia* of 1561 by Jacopo Gastaldi.

4 The Ottoman atlas of Katib Celebi printed in Istanbul in 1732 is largely based on these Dutch and Belgian maps and has no relevance to our subject.

5 Cortesão, *Monumenta*, vol. 2, p. 216 has a photograph of this chart.

The beginning of Dutch cartography

The history of the cartography of the Gulf in the Netherlands starts with a Dutchman, Jan Huygen van Linschoten, who was in Portuguese service in Goa, long before the first voyages of the Dutch East India Company. He saw a map made by a local cartographer in Goa, and on returning to Holland, published it in his book, which was first printed in 1596. The map has Doguada (Aguada) and Sas (a mistake; what is meant is the place called Sar on Portuguese maps). In one respect it is quite an interesting map: in contrast to the other printed maps of this period, it presents Qatar as a small peninsula. This knowledge was soon lost, for with one exception all European maps before 1820 have a distorted view of the Gulf without the Qatar peninsula.

NATOLIAE PARS
MAR DE SALA, vel de Bachu, olim Caspium.
ARMENIA
Caldaran campus
MARIS MEDITERRANEI PARS
CYPRUS
SYRIA
DIARBECH olim Mesopotamia
ASSYRIA
ASIA
CVSISTAN olim Susiana
CHALDEA
ARABIA DESERTA
PARTHIA
PERSIA
FARS
Sinus Persicus
AEGYPTUS
AYAMAN
MARE RUBRUM
MAR ROXO
ARABIA FELIX
TROPICUS CANCRI
MARE ARABICUM ET INDICUM
AFRICAE PARS
DAFRILA
BARNAGASSO
GANFRILA
DANGALI
ADEL
MAGADOXO
Cacorora
Maldivae Insulae
AEQUINOCTIALIS
Henricus F. ab Langren Sculpsit

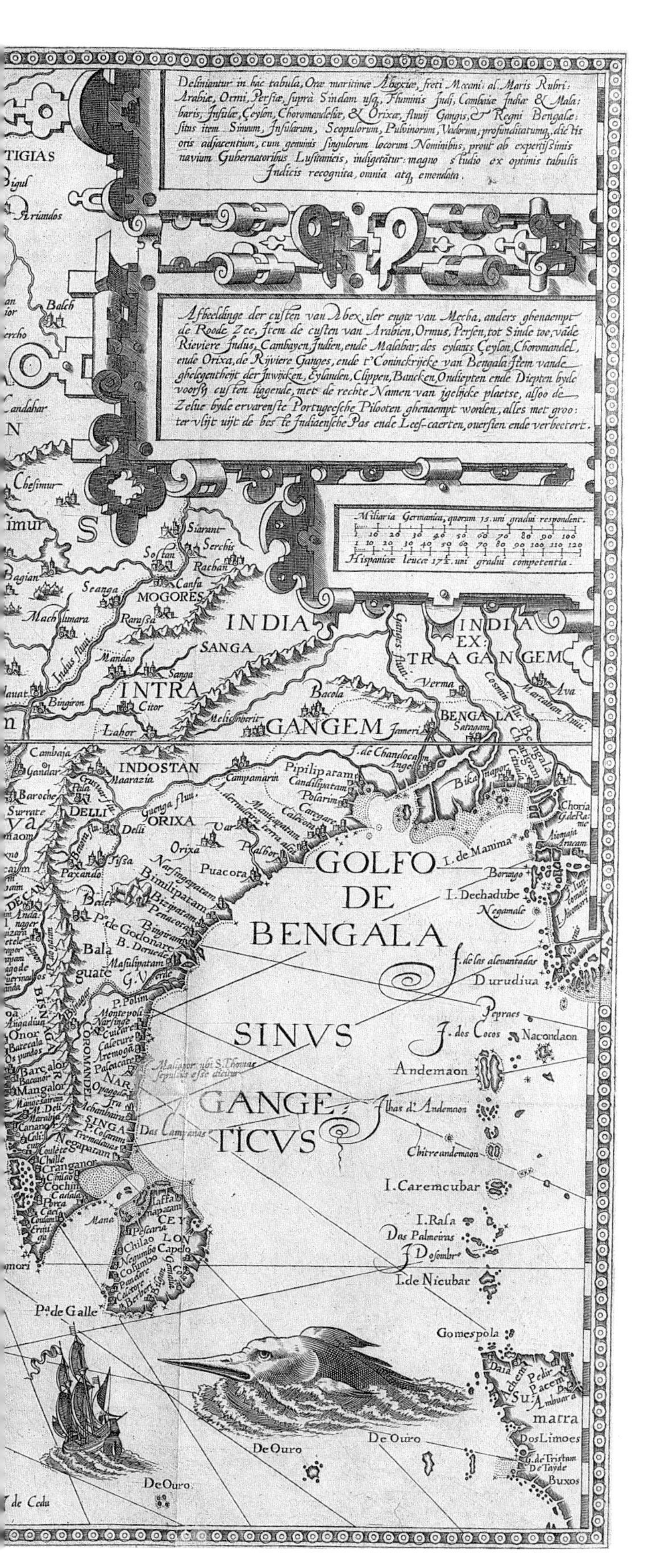

Plate 1

The map of the Western part of Asia published by Jan Huygen van Linschoten. View of the whole.
(Library of the General State Archives of The Netherlands)

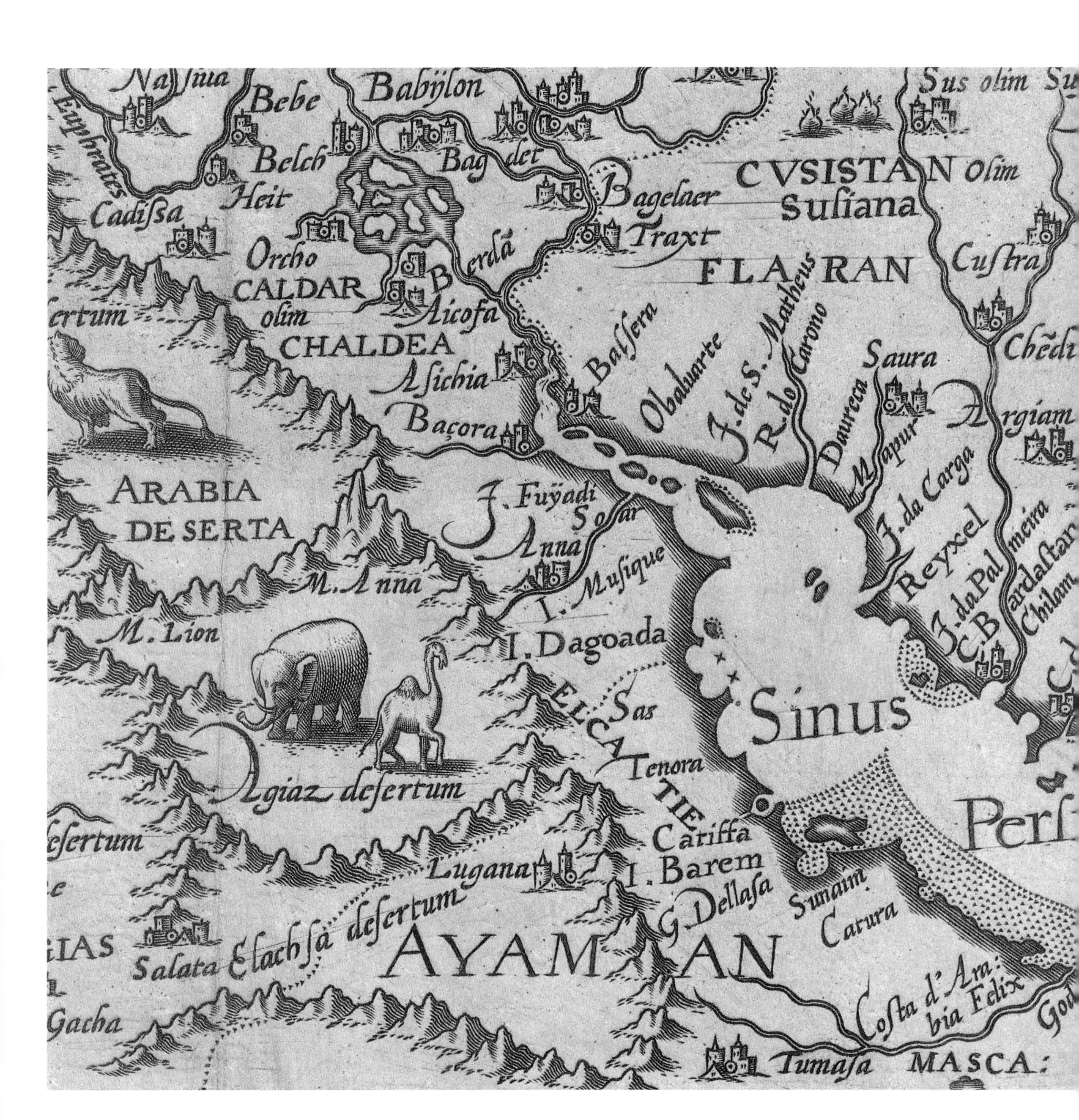
Babylon
Bebe
Belch
Heit
Cadissa
Bagdet
Bagelaer
Traxt
CVSISTAN olim
Susiana
FLA RAN
Sus olim
Custra
Orcho
CALDAR
olim
CHALDEA
Aicofa
Asichia
Baçora
Balsera
Obaluarte
I. de S. Matheus
R. do Caromo
Daurca
Saura
Argiam
ARABIA
DE SERTA
I. Fuyadi
Anna
M. Anna
I. Musique
M. Lion
I. Dagoada
I. da Carga
Reyxel
I. da Palmeira
Sinus
Sas
Tenora
Agiaz desertum
Catiffa
I. Barem
G. Dellasa
Lugana
Elachsa desertum
Salata
AYAM AN
Gacha
Costa d'Arabia Felix
Tumasa
MASCA:
Pers

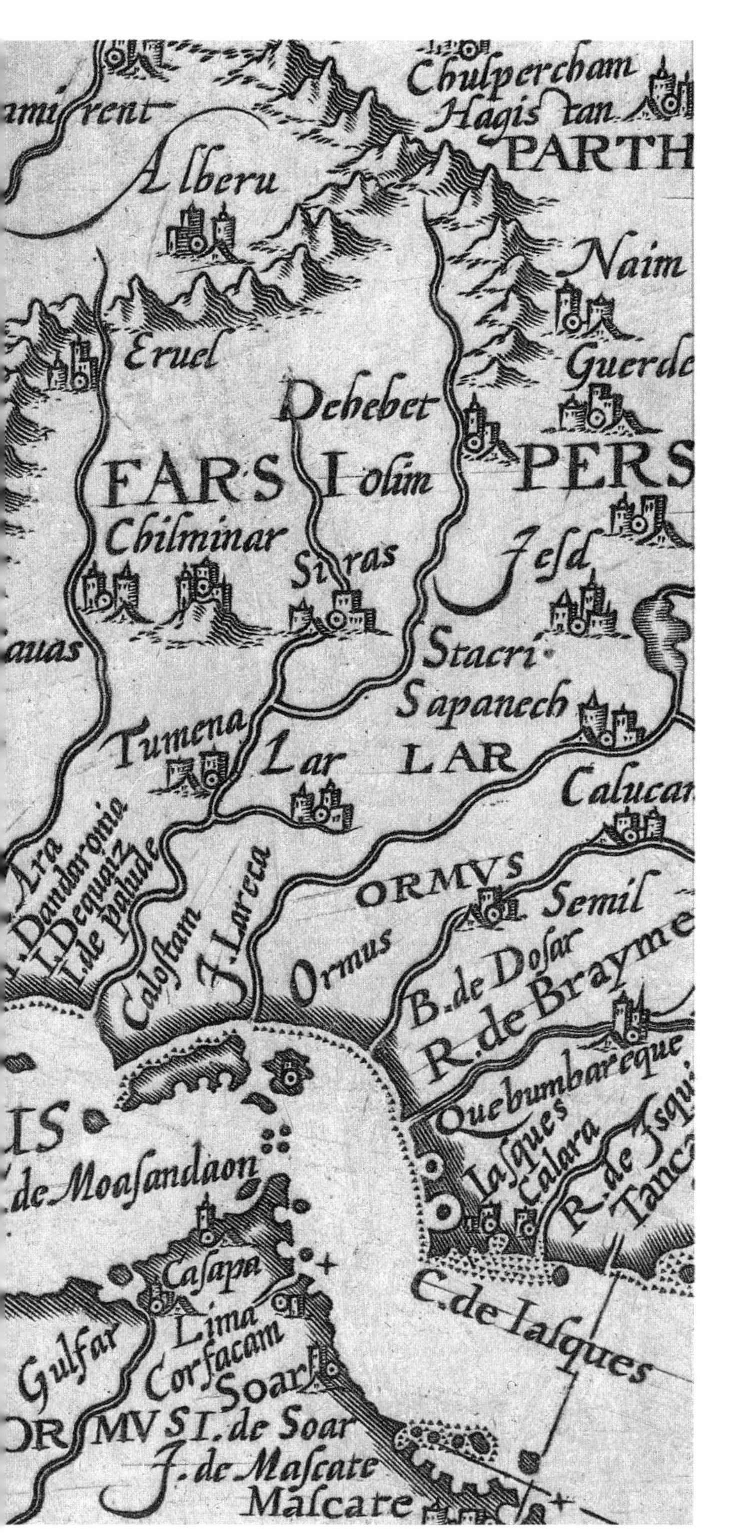

Plate 2

Linschoten's map of 1596: detail.
(Library of the General State Archives of The Netherlands)

The first Dutch expedition to Basra

In the year 1645, two small Dutch ships, the *Delfshaven* and the *Schelvis*, set out from Bandar Abbas on their first trading mission to Basra. Only small ships could be used to reach Basra. Three log-books of this expedition can be found in the General State Archives of The Netherlands.[6] One of these log-books was published in a Dutch geographic periodical in 1907 by A. Hotz.[7] The leader of the expedition, Captain Cornelis Cornelisz. Roobacker, commanding officer of the *Delfshaven*, made a map, which has survived among the papers of the Dutch East India Company official Artus Gijsels, now kept among the manuscripts of the Badische Landesbibliothek in Karlsruhe.[8] Hotz did not know the Karlsruhe chart, and when publishing the log-book added, as an illustration, a Dutch nautical chart of the Gulf from the collection of the Leiden University Library. He attributes this chart to Roobacker, but marks on the Golf of Oman show that this particular chart was made after the Dutch expedition to Oman of 1666. The Leiden chart is much like the nautical chart reproduced on plate 7.

Roobacker's ships had English charts on board, but Roobacker complained that they were very inaccurate. As was the custom for shipping to Basra, the Dutch ships took a local pilot on board on Kharg island. The pilot took the ships directly to the Shatt al Arab, but there trouble began. The Shatt al Arab was very shallow at that time, and only dhows, engaged in coastal traffic between Basra and Bahrain, often under Portuguese flag, could navigate their way through. For this reason, the Shatt al Arab was called the Bahrain river at the time. The Dutch entered the Shatt al Arab, but did not dare to proceed. They then returned, and instead of turning to the North, where the Bamishir (now the river which gives access to the Persian port of Abadan) provided access to Basra for larger ships, turned to the South. They entered another very shallow passage: the Khor Abdallah. Finding no way through, they turned South along the coast of Bubiyan, where they tried to turn about again, probably at Fasht al Aych. Finding no safe entrance, they set out in a boat to some low sandbanks, probably near Bubiyan, but there they found nothing, although here and there they saw fishing boats from afar. Finally, they returned to the North and found the entrance of the Bamishir.
Roobacker made a chart of his travels between Laraq and Basra, with marks of depths and accurate notes on geographic latitude. This chart shows his progress up to Bubiyan.

[6] The log-books can be found in the private archive of Wollebrand Geleynssen de Jongh, nos. 280a-c.
[7] A. Hotz, Cornelis Cornelisz. Roobackers' scheepjournaal Gamron-Basra (1645), *Tijdschrift van het Koninklijk Nederlands Aardrijkskundig Genootschap*, 2nd series vol. 24 (1507), pp. 289–405. This contains the text of the logbook no. 280a only.
[8] Artus Gijsels papers 478.

Of the three logbooks of this expedition which have survived of this expedition, we give a translation of Roobacker's text, which was published in 1907. If one of the other logbooks gives significant clarification, this has been mentioned between brackets.

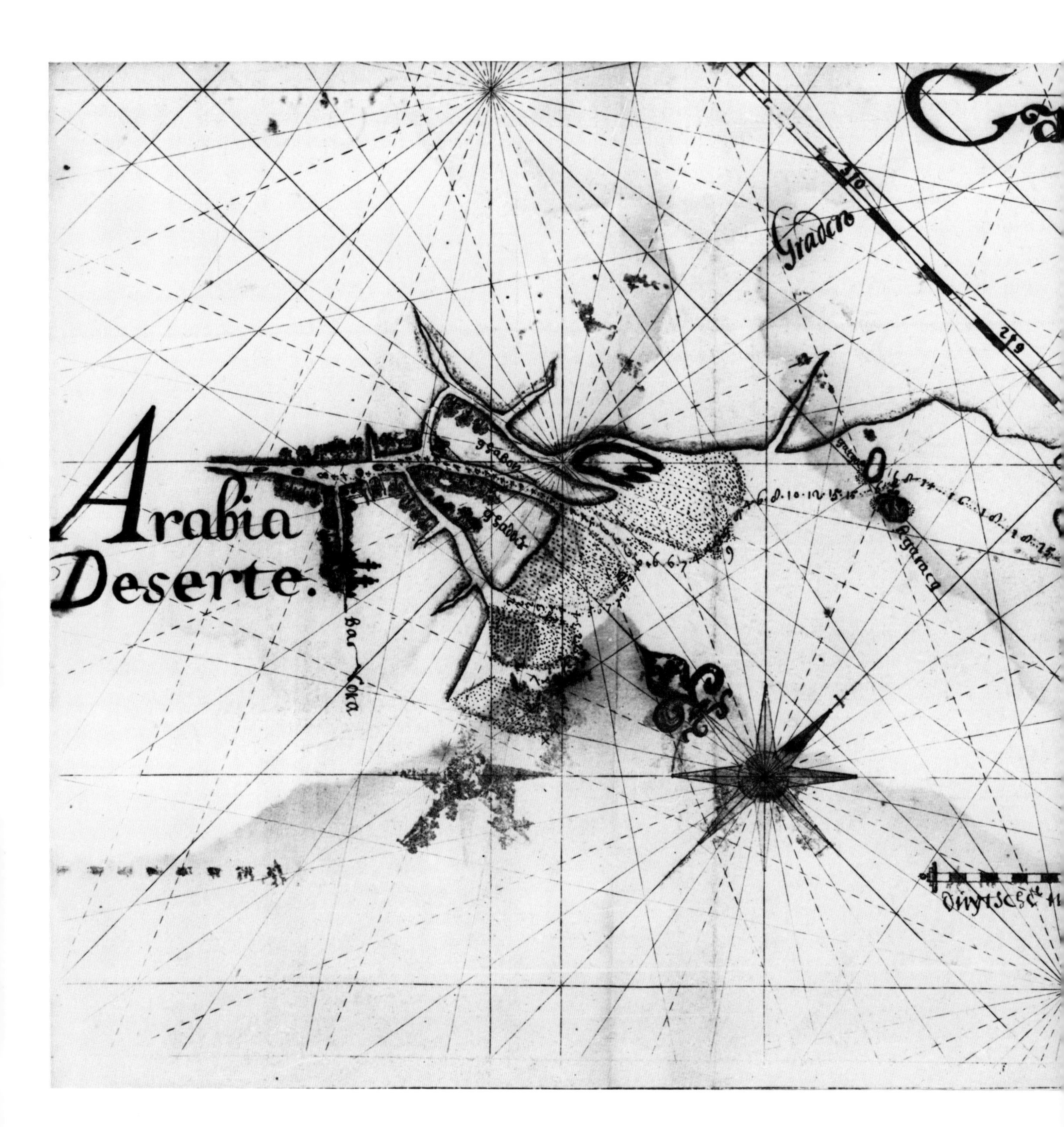
Arabia
Deserte.
Graden

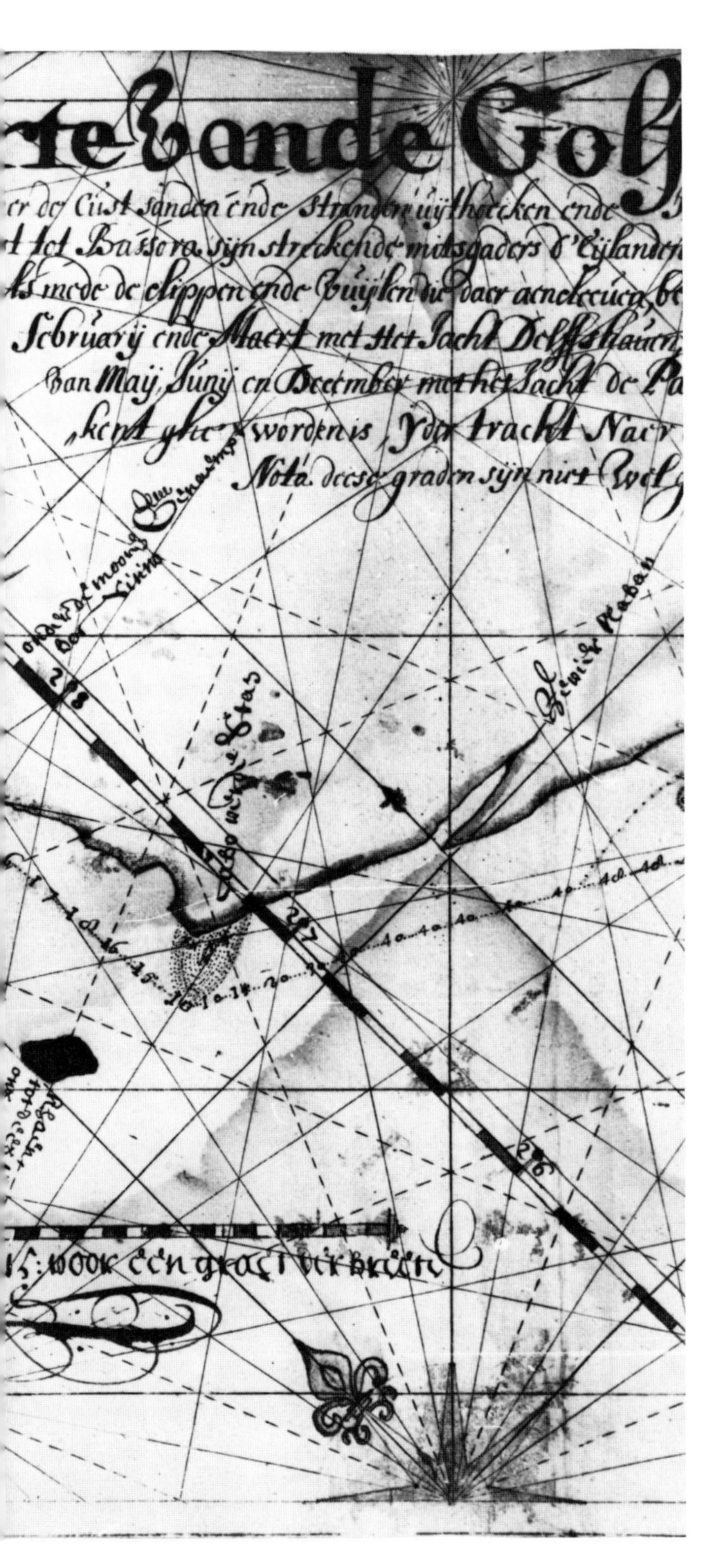

Plate 3

Western sheet of the sketch of the route taken by the Dutch ships on their way to Basra in 1645.
(Badische Landesbibliothek Karlsruhe, Artus Gijsels papers 478)

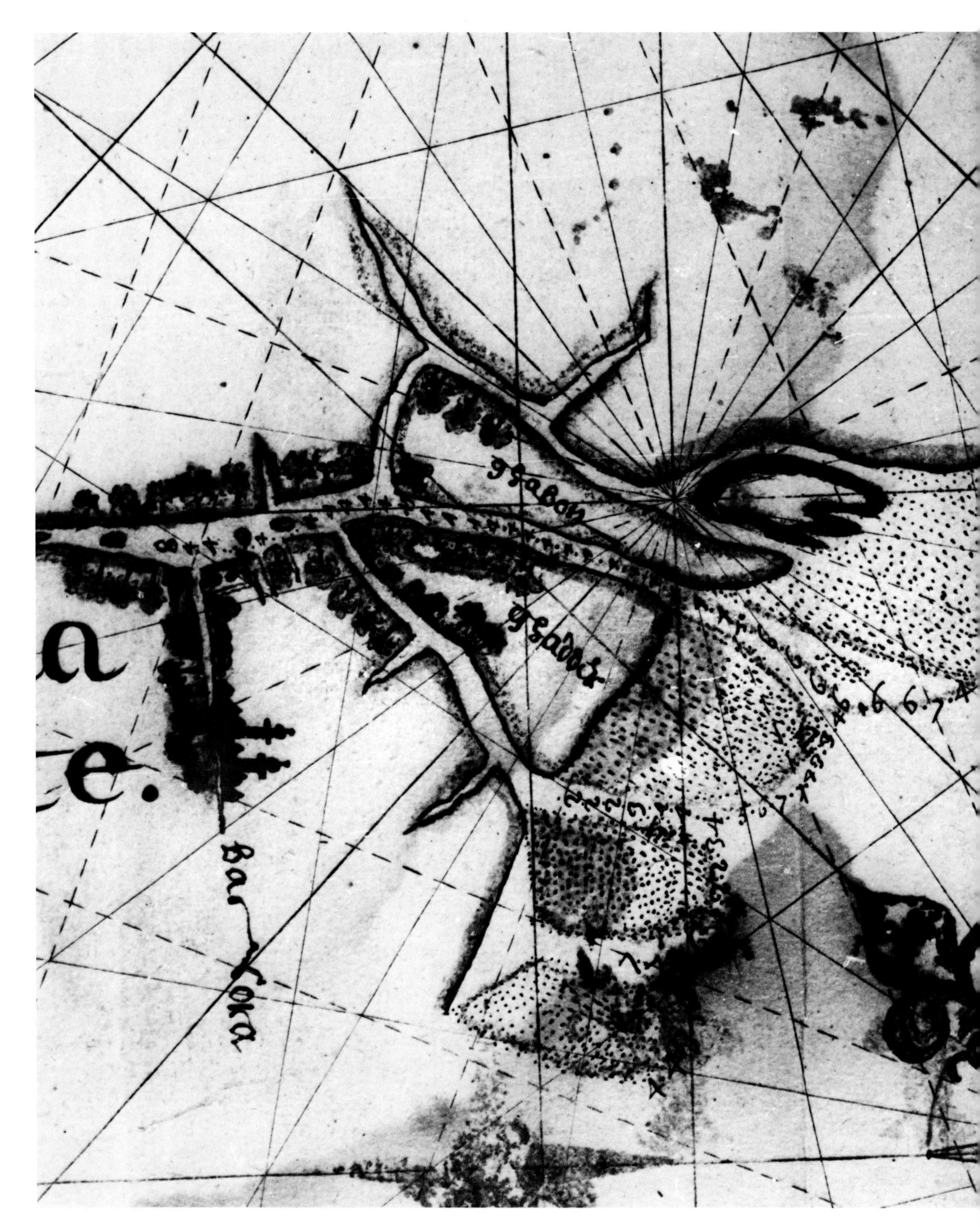

Plate 4

Detail of the map on plate 3 showing the soundings made between Kharg, Bubiyan and Basra. Dutch handwriting of the seventeenth century may not be easy to read. The ships came from the right-hand side of the chart between Kgarack [Kharg] and Gargu [Khargu]. The Dutch ship first crossed the extremity of the shallows off Ghaban [Qubban], but, once there, did not enter by the right entrance. Instead they sailed around the shallows off Ghadder [Khidr]. They tried to enter the Shatt al Arab, but found it too shallow. Turning back they tried two lower entrances between the mudflats: the Khor Abdallah and a creek near Fasht al Aych. Finally they turned back, entering the Bamishir, as shown by the long line of depth figures.

doen is zijn boote weder aen boort gecomen, conde het landt gemackelijck sien, op dato heeft den coopm. Dirck Sarcerius de witte vlagge laten waijen, om den raedt aen boort te hebben, waer op datelyck daer nae toe gevaren zijn, aen boort gecomen zijnde, heeft den voorn. coopm. Sarcerius den raet voorgedragen, offe niet geraetsaem soude wesen, dat men de boote wel gemant naer landt soude senden, omme te vernemen off een ander man conde becomen, die ons inde revier soude connen brengen, offe selve conde vinden, want de lootsen ons het compas tot 3 a 4 maels het compas hadde doen rondt zeylen, en tot noch toe geen teecken offe eenige kennisse conde wijsen, en ons dickwils liet ancker winden en datelyck weder setten, en ons den 19 passado verclaert hadde wel bekent te zijn, en als nu geen kennisse en hadde, gelyck dagelijcx blyckt, en de E. comp. schepen en goederen in groot perikel stonden, soo is naer dat den raedt t geproponeerde van Sr. Sarcerius, alles wel en rypelyck overwogen hebbende, en met een parige stemme besloten, als bij resolutie is blyckende, zijn doen weder naer boort toe gevaren, aldoen heeft Delffshaven zijn prouw van boort gesonden om te [illegible], tegen den avondt als wanneer de vloedt begon te gaen, soo is de boote van Delffshaven naer landt toe gevaren, [illegible] doen daer 5 glasen uyt waren, begon de ebbe sterck te gaen en styff te coelen, soo dat outrent een cleijn [illegible] schoot wech gedreven zijn, hebben daer op noch een ancker laten vallen bleven geanckert leggen tot smorgens

Abij 22 smorgens goedt weder doch betogen lucht, het luchjen vande N.O. sagen weder 3 vaertuygen offe barcken onder het landt, hebben onse ancker gelicht en zijn onder zeyl gegaen om weder bij de admirael te comen, hebben het by hem neder geset, de vloedt begon hart te gaen, outrent te negen uren, hebben 2 barcken gesien int N.N.O. van ons, waer op Sr. Sarcerius zijn [illegible] aen ons boort gesonden heeft, en belast dat wij onse schuyt wel gemandt nevens de prauw soude senden nae de vaertuyge toe om te besien, offe daer een man conde becomen, die ons inde revier brocht, doch de windt begon vande Z. t loopen en ooc N. [illegible] en begon een moije coelte op te waijen, soo dat niet bij haer conde comen, waer op dat zij weer naer boort toe zijn gekeert

Abij 23 smorgens goedt weder betogen lucht doch stilletjens met den dach hebben de boote van Delffshaven int N.W. van ons gesien met noch een ander vaertuych, maer conde niet nae ons toe comen, door dien dat de vloedt hardt ginck, waer op dat zij haer dregge mosten laten vallen, om de ebbe t'verwachten, waer op Sr. Sarcerius de prouw nae haer toe gesonden heeft, om den ondercoopm. vander Campen, nevens den opperstierm. Cornelis Haert te laten halen uit de boote, want wij naer haer verlangden, outrent de middach is de prau met den voornoemden ondercoopman, met den opperstierm., met een loots, die selve een vaertuych met hem brochten, aen ons boort gecomen, door oorsaeck dat Sr. Sarcerius aldier aen boort was, hebben ons verhaelt dat al in de revier geweest waren, tot bij een dorp, daer zy de lootsman van daen gehadt hadden, outrent 1 a 2 uren nae de middach quam de boote met het andere vaertuych aen boort op dato heeft de lootsman belast dat men het ancker soude lichten, om met de ebbe weder uit te zeylen, dat wij ingecomen waren, hebben onse ancker datelyck gelicht en zijn onder zeyl gegaen en hebben het weder uyt gelaveert, streckende meest O.Z.O. en W.N.W. 3 glasen voor sons ondergauck waren boven de oostelycxste

Plate 5 Page from the log-book of the *Rijnsburg*, one of the two ships on Roobacker's expedition, with the events of 21–23 July 1645. (General State Archives of The Netherlands, Geleynssen de Jong no. 280b)

The text of the log-book of the *Delfshaven* by Captain Roobacker shows how difficult it was for Europeans to find their way in the shallow waters of the Upper Gulf. We quote here the text in Roobacker's own log-book of 20–23 July 1645. On the 20th, the Dutch ships were between the shallows, just outside the entrance to the Shatt al Arab.

20 July
We often saw small boats come down the river, but we could not approach them to ask the way. Later in the morning the wind turned WSW, and in the afternoon there was a little wind SSW. After low tide we sailed to the West. The land is all low there, and there are no landmarks; it stretches WSW. Because of the shallow banks, one has to stay one and a half miles away from the bank, and even there, at high tide there is no more than two or two-and-a-half fathoms of water; then we met with a clay bottom at three to four fathoms. Sometimes it is difficult to distinguish the land from the water. The pilot led us to a place where there was only two fathoms of water and getting shallower all the time. Against the advice of the pilot we dropped anchor because we had no more water under the ship and low tide was coming. We were afraid that we would not be able to get off there anymore, and as far as we could see, we had the river WNW about three and a half miles away. At sunset we lifted anchor again to get into deeper water away from the bank, because we had heard that the water, given a normal tide, goes up and down by nine feet. [They were turning back then; according to the log-book of the First Mate of the *Schelvis*, no. 280 c, at that moment they were 1.5 miles off the Southern point of Khidr.] We sailed SSE in light wind, while the incoming tide held us back. In the evening, when high tide was ending, we dropped anchor at five fathoms and stayed there the night. We found that a SSE moon causes high tide here. We could not get any knowledge of the land, although we were near the bank and in front of the river.
On the 21st at first daylight the wind was N by W and the tide came up NW. We went NW by N, at depths of five to ten fathoms, even as much as twelve fathoms. We turned about until we got to a three-fathom deep clay bottom. We thought that we were at the right place, but at low ebb we saw that we were wrong and that we had entered a wrong channel between the shallows on the eastern side of the creek. It was very shallow. We tacked about at five to five-and-a-half fathoms and we saw some small hills on the land, which were fisheries at the entry to the river. Our pilot still had no idea what to do and so we dropped anchor down the creek at six fathoms and called the council together.[9] We decided to find another pilot as soon as possible, because the one we had taken on at Kharg had led us astray three to four times and because he had no knowledge of the land or shallows. For three days we had searched up and down and we saw no opening nor did we get any knowledge from the pilot about the land or the river. So a decision was taken to send out Undermerchant Nicolaas van der Cappen and First Mate Cornelis Crijnen 't

[9] The minutes of this meeting can be found in: General State Archives of The Netherlands, Geleynssen de Jongh papers, no. 280d.

Hardt with a boat, to see if they could find another good pilot to bring the Company's ships and people safely inside the river. This decision was taken because we had no help from our pilot who said that he had lost his way. We sent our boat, well-manned and with Van der Cappen and First Mate 't Hardt landwards as it was not wise to keep sailing from side to side, nor to turn around between shallows with such precious small ships and rich cargo on board. In the evening at high tide we sent the boat away.

On the morning of the 22nd there was a light wind from WNW; we saw five small boats sailing before the wind towards the river, wanting to enter. We sent our small boat, and the boat belonging to the *Schelvis* to ask them the way, but they went so fast that the small boats could not catch up with them, so they returned. With the small boat we found that NE from us it was three to three-and-a-half fathoms at low tide. Half a mile from us we saw a long surf lying to the East, and to the West, two small banks above water which the boat belonging to the Schelvis sailed to, but they found nothing but mud and shallows. [According to the log-book 280c, observation of the First Mate of the *Schelvis*, they were at that moment at a latitude of 29 degrees 48 minutes, which means that they were at Fasht al Aych near the Eastern extremity of Bubiyan.][10]

[10] Hotz, 'Roobackers' scheepsjournaal,' pp. 367–369; the original of this journal is Geleynsen de Jongh papers no. 280a.

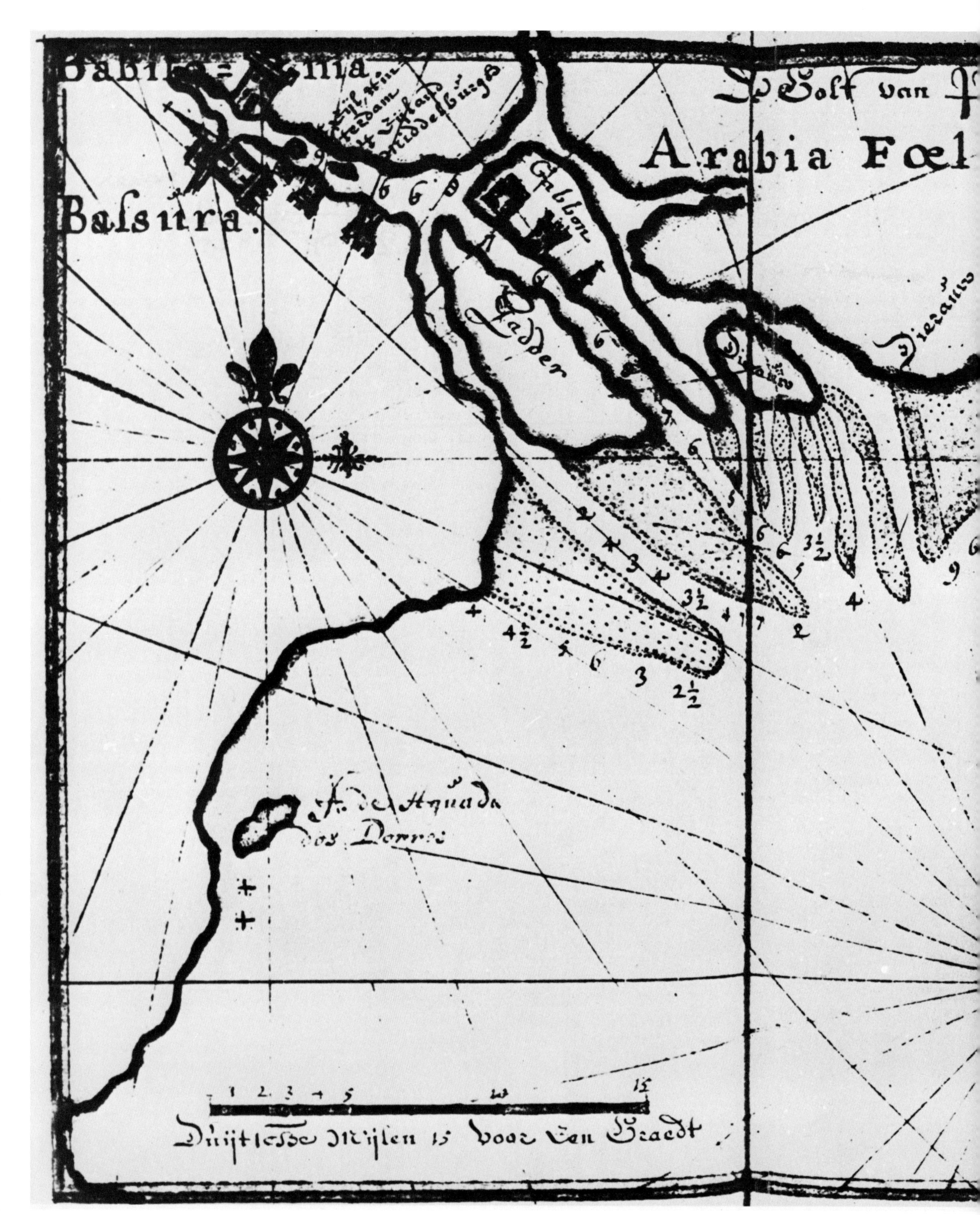
Basora
Arabia Fœl
Golf van
Gabbon
Padder
Duytsche Mijlen 15 voor een Graedt

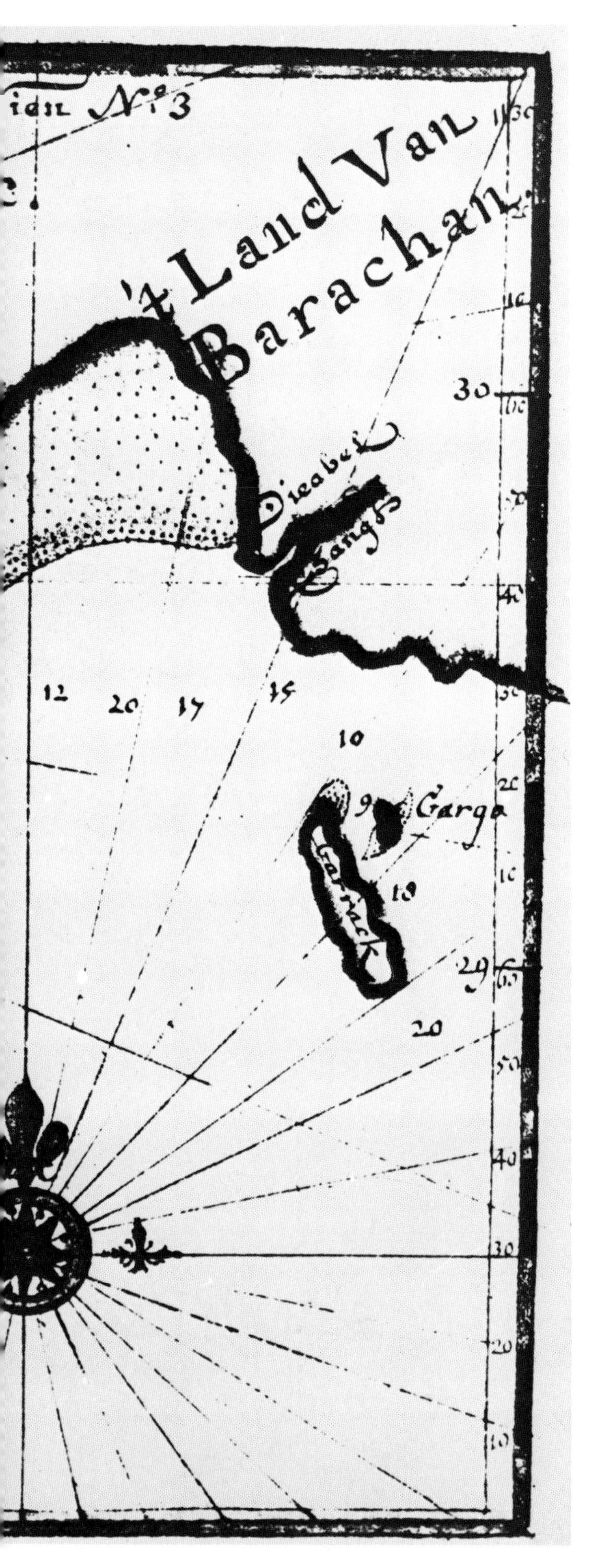

Plate 6

The British Library in London has a small Dutch atlas, probably from the collection of a Director of the Dutch East India Company, in which there are maps of the Upper, Central and Lower parts of the Gulf. It is the first Dutch attempt to compile the available cartographic data on the Gulf. It should be dated between 1645 and 1666. The presence of warning signs near Ilha de Aguada shows that European ships had passed through.
(British Library, Add. Mss. 34184)

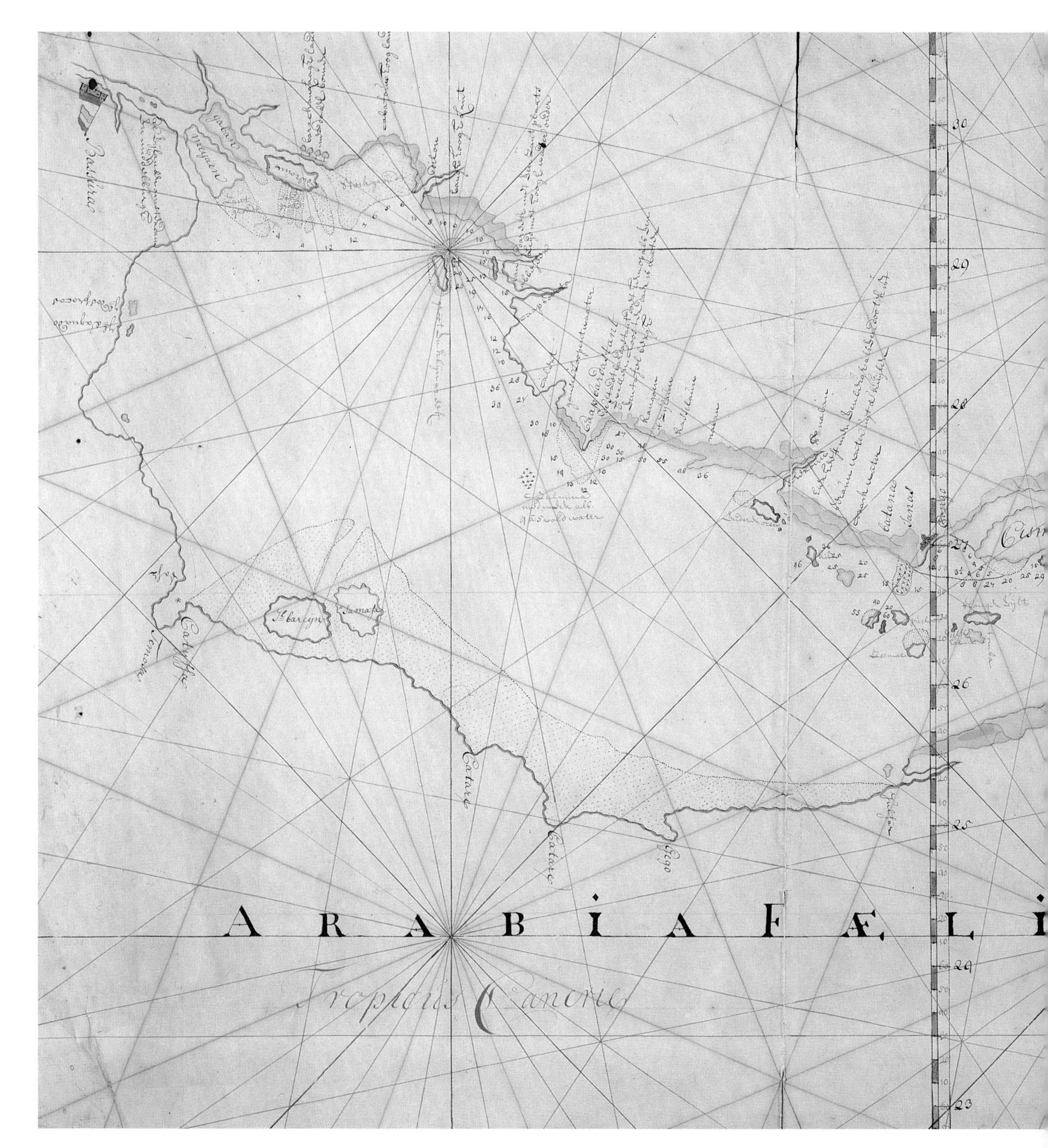
ARABIA FÆLI
Tropicus Cancri

Plate 7

The classical nautical chart of the Gulf as produced by the Dutch East India Company. This is the most beautiful of several examples of this chart which have survived. The English chart of the Gulf, published by John Thornton, *English Pilot* 3rd book, behind p. 34, in 1703 is a later version of this chart.
(General State Archives of The Netherlands, Maps and Drawings Department VEL 220)

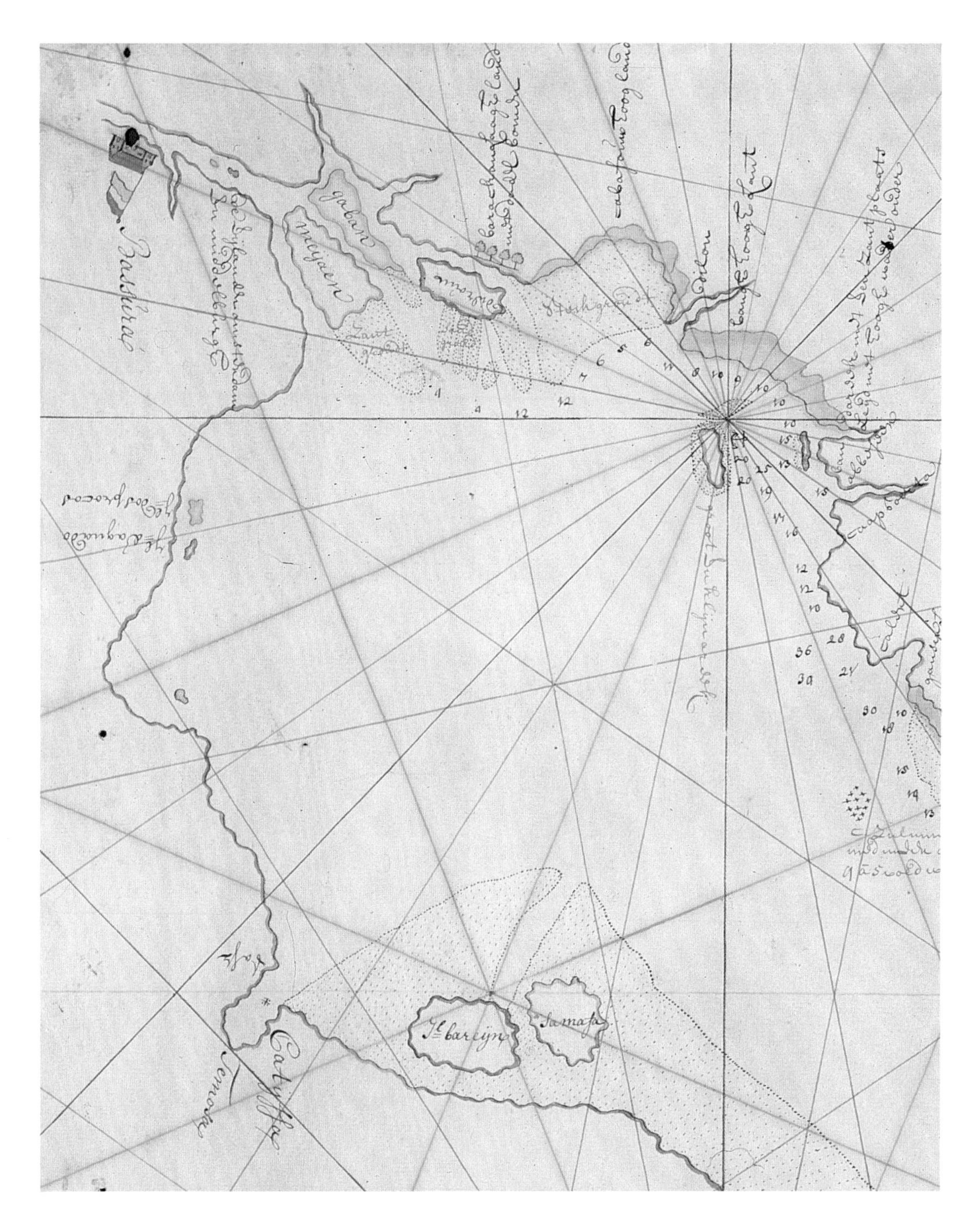

Plate 8 Detail of plate 7. On Kuwaiti territory Ilha de Aguada and Dos Porcos are visible.

Plate 9

Vingboons's map of the Arabian peninsula of c. 1660. This map is a combination of data from Linschoten's map with data from other currents in Portuguese cartography. It has Aguada as well as Dos Porcos, and is a particularly fine example of the map-maker's art.
(General State Archives of The Netherlands, Maps and Drawings Department VELH 219.10)

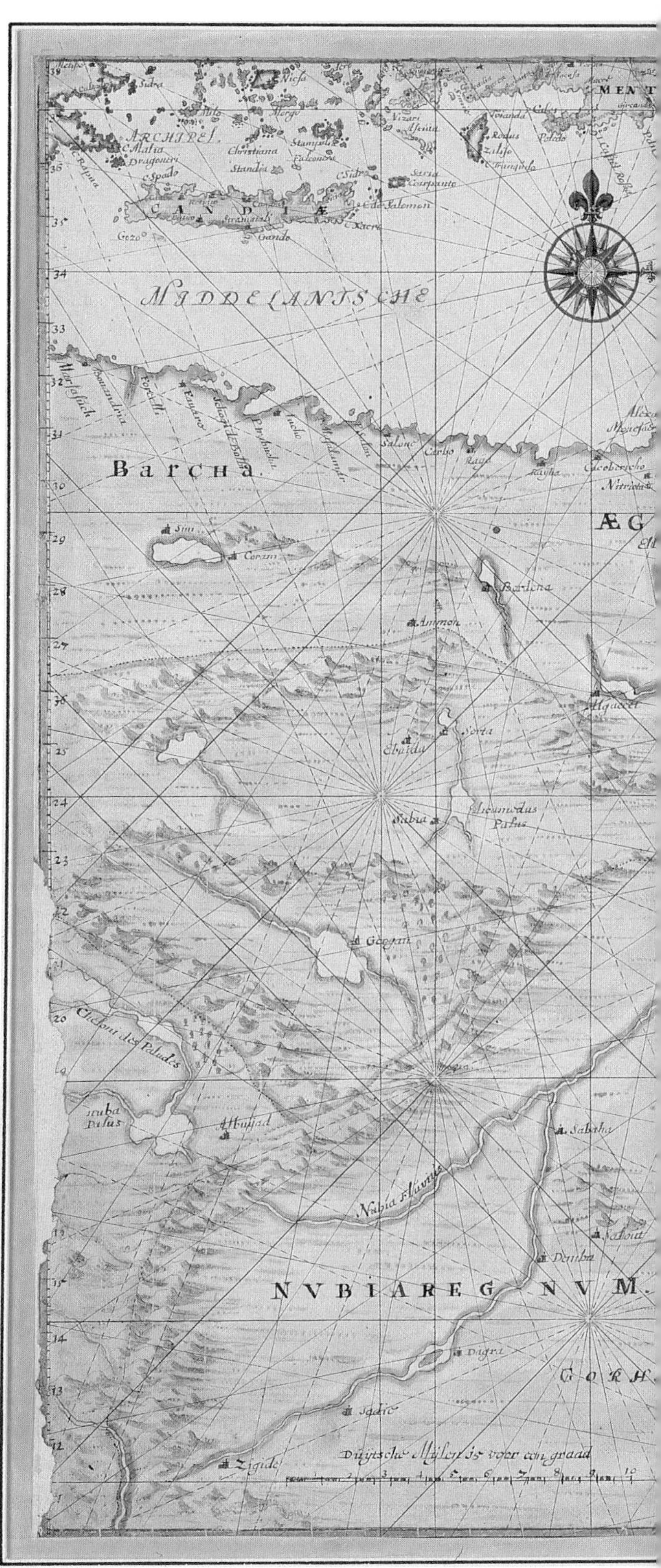

Plate 10

Detail of plate 9.

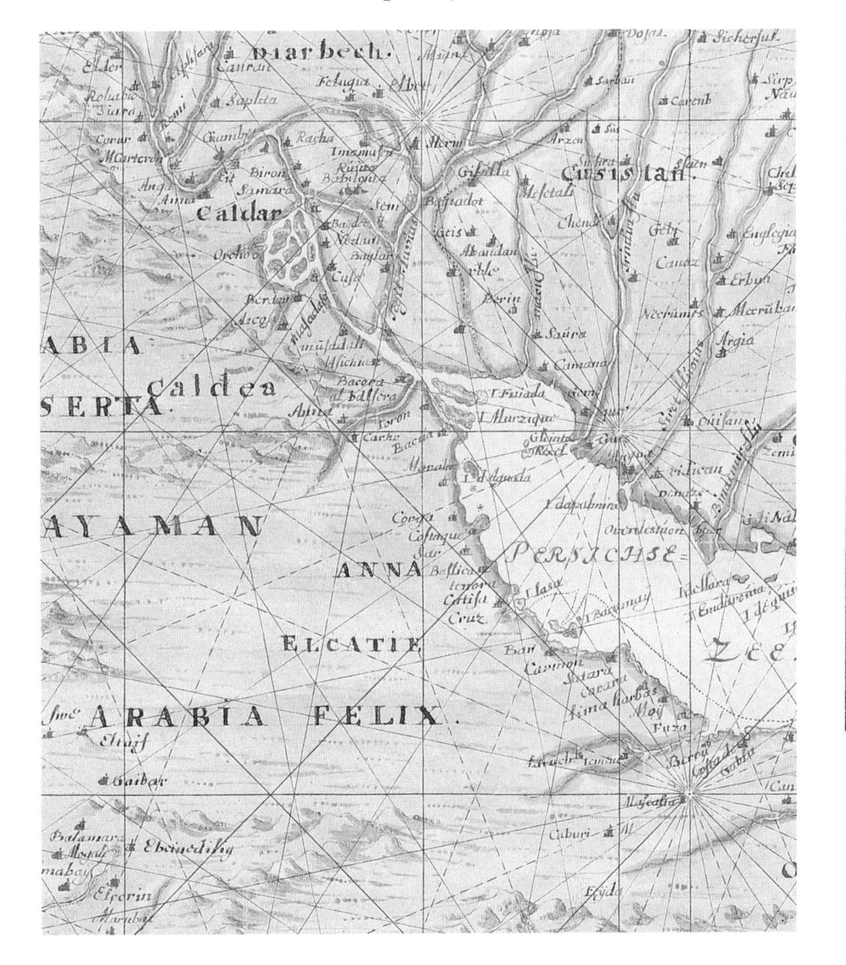

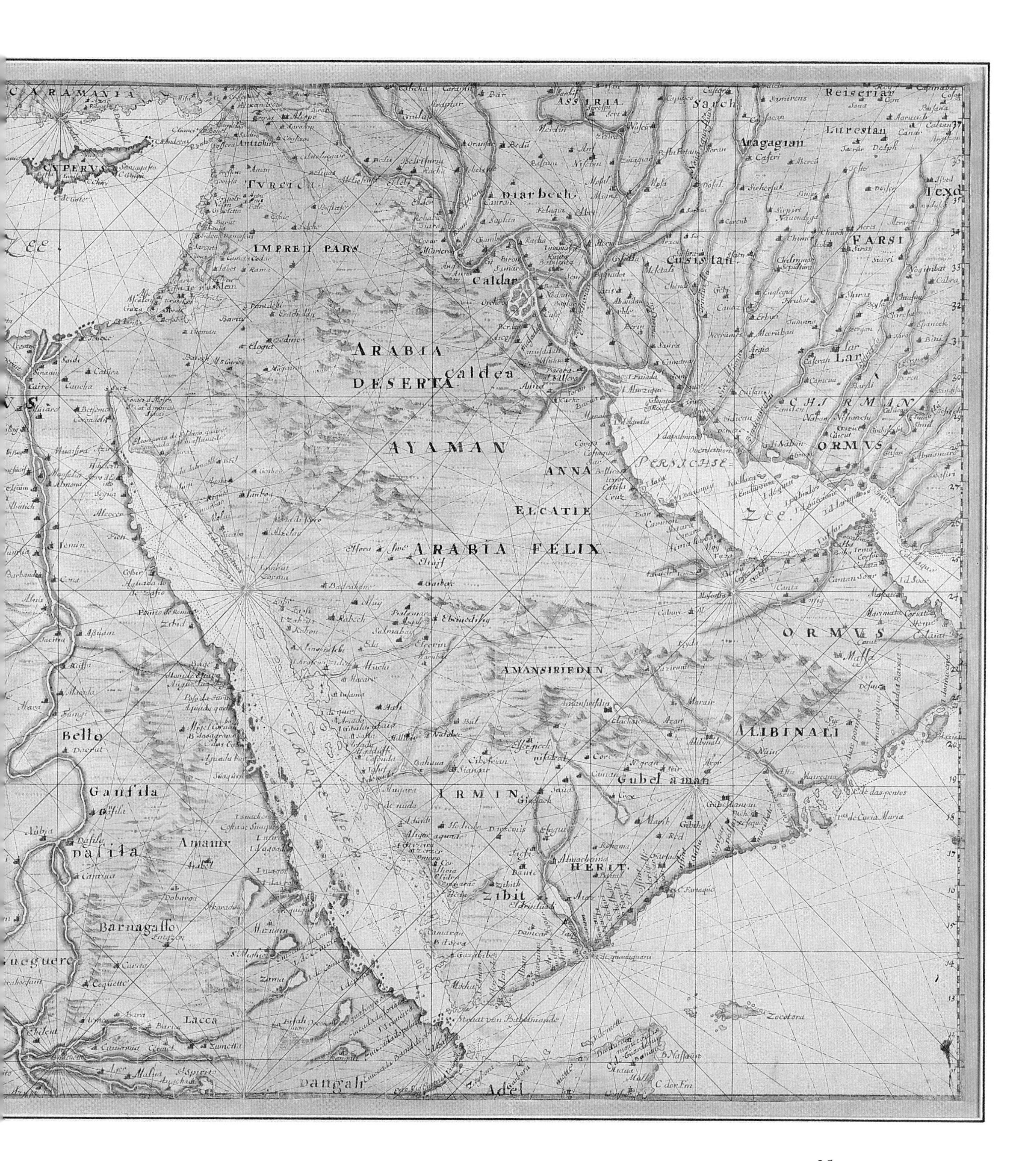
CARAMANIA
CYPERVS
ASSIRIA
Reiseriar
Lurestan
Aragagian
Diarbech
Caldar
IMPREIJ PARS
Cusistan
FARSI
ARABIA DESERTA
Caldea
CHIRMAN
ORMVS
AYAMAN
ANNA
ELCATIE
ARABIA FELIX
ZEE
AMANSIRIEDEN
ALIBINALI
Bello
IRMIN
Gubel aman
Ganfila
Amanr
HERIT
Zibit
Barnagasso
Lacca
Zocotora
Adel

A chart with the Gulf of Kuwait?

The chart shown on plate 11, a printed French nautical chart published in 1692 by Pierre Mortier, an Amsterdam publisher of maps of French origin, must have been of doubtful value to sailors. The map was printed in Holland and mixes some topographic data from good sources (maybe Van Linschoten?) with the bad geometry common to the cartographic tradition of Ortelius. In comparison with other charts like no. 7, it gives a very distorted image. Although it carries compass-lines, its lack of geometric accuracy makes it more like a geographical map. Nevertheless it presents a rather original image of the Kuwait area. It shows the traditional image of the borders of the Ottoman provinces, showing the Eastern area of Saudi Arabia as Bahrain province: the administrative situation in the 1550's. On the other hand, it shows this province as largely dominated by the Emir of Qatif, which shows adaptation to the political situation of the 1660's. Of considerable interest is the fact that this map is the first to clearly show Kuwait Bay (without putting a name to it). Also interesting is its use of the traditional Portuguese names in connection with Kuwait.
It is difficult to see on which sources this chart is based. On the one hand there is its manifestly primitive character, on the other hand there are some strangely accurate data: the placing of Aguada Island in exactly the same position as Faylaka—at the entrance of the Gulf of Kuwait. We may presume that this was originally a Portuguese geographical map, which was to a certain extent updated (with new information possibly received from Carmelite monks in Basra, although the way the drawing of the rivers below Basra were executed seems to be too inaccurate for this source).
This map also shows a particularity which is quite common in European maps of the seventeenth and eighteenth centuries. On such maps, there is a large river flowing between Basra and Al Hasa. This fabulous river originates from a misunderstanding of an important travellers account, that of the Venetian Gasparo Balbi in the year 1580.[11] Balbi recounts that trade from Basra can take two routes. The first is by way of the river called Hormuz and was used by large ships sailing to India. The second was called the river of Bahrain and was used by small craft sailing to Bahrain and Al Hasa. Balbi's river of Bahrain is the Shatt al Arab, which was so shallow that it could not be used by larger ships sailing to India. In the seventeenth century, they used the Bamishir instead, as Roobacker's ships did. Cartographers did not understand Balbi's story very well and invented their own 'River of Bahrain' which brought the ships all the way to that island.
One of the sources of this chart may have been a Portuguese manuscript chart, a very special type of chart dating back to c. 1680, which is now to be seen in Capetown. We have not seen more than a rather hazy photograph of this map, but it clearly shows the

[11] Gasparo Balbi, *Viaggi*, pp. 111–112.

Gulf of Kuwait with a name at the place where Mortier's chart has Sar. Behind the Gulf of Kuwait (where Jahra is now to be found), the name of a place is visible, but it is illegible on the published photograph.[12]

[12] Anonymous manuscript chart of the coasts of the Arabian peninsula from the Library of Groote Schuur, Capetown, no. R 912 AFR; photograph in Teixeira da Mota, *Cartas Portuguesas*, fig. 10.

Plate II Pierre Mortier, *Carte particulière d'une partie d'Asie où sont les îles Maledives...* French chart, derived from Dutch and Portuguese prototypes.
(General State Archives of The Netherlands, Maps and Drawings Department, MCAL 3880)

Part 2
KAZIMA

In 1652, a map appeared in France which showed a place called Kadhema. This seems to stand for Kazima, a locality of Kuwait. On the map, this place is clearly placed outside the borders of the Ottoman province of Iraq. At first, Kazima was rather inaccurately positioned, but later, from c. 1730 onwards, maps improved.

Plate 12

The oldest Sanson map of Arabia, *Carte de l'Arabie pétrée, déserte et heureuse* of 1652. (Collection of Dr. Sultan bin Muhammad Al-Qasimi)

In the year 1652, the French geographer Nicolas Sanson published a map with the title *Carte de l'Arabie pétrée, déserte et heureuse*. On this map, there is a small place called Kadhima in the Arabian desert, outside the border of the province of Iraq. On the map dated 1652, this place is wrongly positioned, but this improves on later maps, where Kadhema or Kazima (or on scholarly maps Cathema) is situated in Kuwait. In fact, when I first discovered Kazima on a historical map, it was in an eighteenth-century map where Kazima is often drawn as a very sizeable place on the site of Kuwait. Searching backwards from this initial point, I found that earlier maps put Kazima slightly more inland and that Sanson's map was the first to have the name.

In modern Kuwait, the name Kazima was still known for an area on the Northern coast of the Gulf of Kuwait, not far from Jahra in a north-easterly direction. In 1654, a new version of Sanson's map was published, this time with the title *Carte des Trois Arabies*. It seems to correct a number of the errors found in the first version. One of these corrections is that Cathema is nearer to the coast, while clearly remaining outside the borders of the province of Iraq. Other editions of maps by Sanson do not show Kazima at all, e.g. the edition by Jaillot of 1695.

L'ARABIE
PETRÉE, DESERTE,
ET HEVREVSE,
Par le S.r Sanson d'Abb. Geo. du R.
Auec priuil. pour 20. ans.
1652.
MER D'ARABIE.
Æ Peyrounin Sculp.

Plate 13 Enlarged detail of the map on plate 12.

The improved Kazima maps

It is not clear which map was the first to show Cathema, or Kazima, as a coastal place; this was probably done for the first time on one of the maps of the French cartographer Guillaume De l'Isle. De l'Isle's first maps are rather dull copies of Sanson's maps, but later editions are better.[13] A map of Africa dated 1722, which was recently reprinted, is the oldest map known to me showing Cathema on the coast of the Gulf, approximately in the position of modern-day Kuwait.[14] Another innovation on these maps is that Kazima is shown as a relatively important place. Kazima is still situated outside the borders of Ottoman Iraq. Although the geometric drawing of borders on maps was still rather primitive at that time and methods of representation in evolution, the consistent positioning of a place in a set position is a very strong indication that the maps are accurate on this point. Moreover, schemes for the division of the Ottoman Empire into administrative districts had been circulating in Europe since the seventeenth century, and it was known which places belonged to a certain district and which did not.

In later years, many maps appeared which followed the innovations of De l'Isle. These new-style maps relate a number of economic and demographic changes in the area. The following chapter will record these types of changes, but it is still difficult to link them to the evolution of cartography since there are no letters or reports known to me which mention Kazima.

13 A photograph of the first map in Tibbets, *Cartography of Arabia*, plate 14.
14 Tooley, *Collector's Guide to Maps of Africa*, plate 52.

Plate 14

In 1732 the Amsterdam map-maker Isaac Tirion published the first Dutch map to locate Cathema on the coast. It is shown as one of the principal ports of the Gulf. Tirion follows Sanson in putting Kazima clearly outside the borders of Ottoman Iraq. (Collection B.J. Slot)

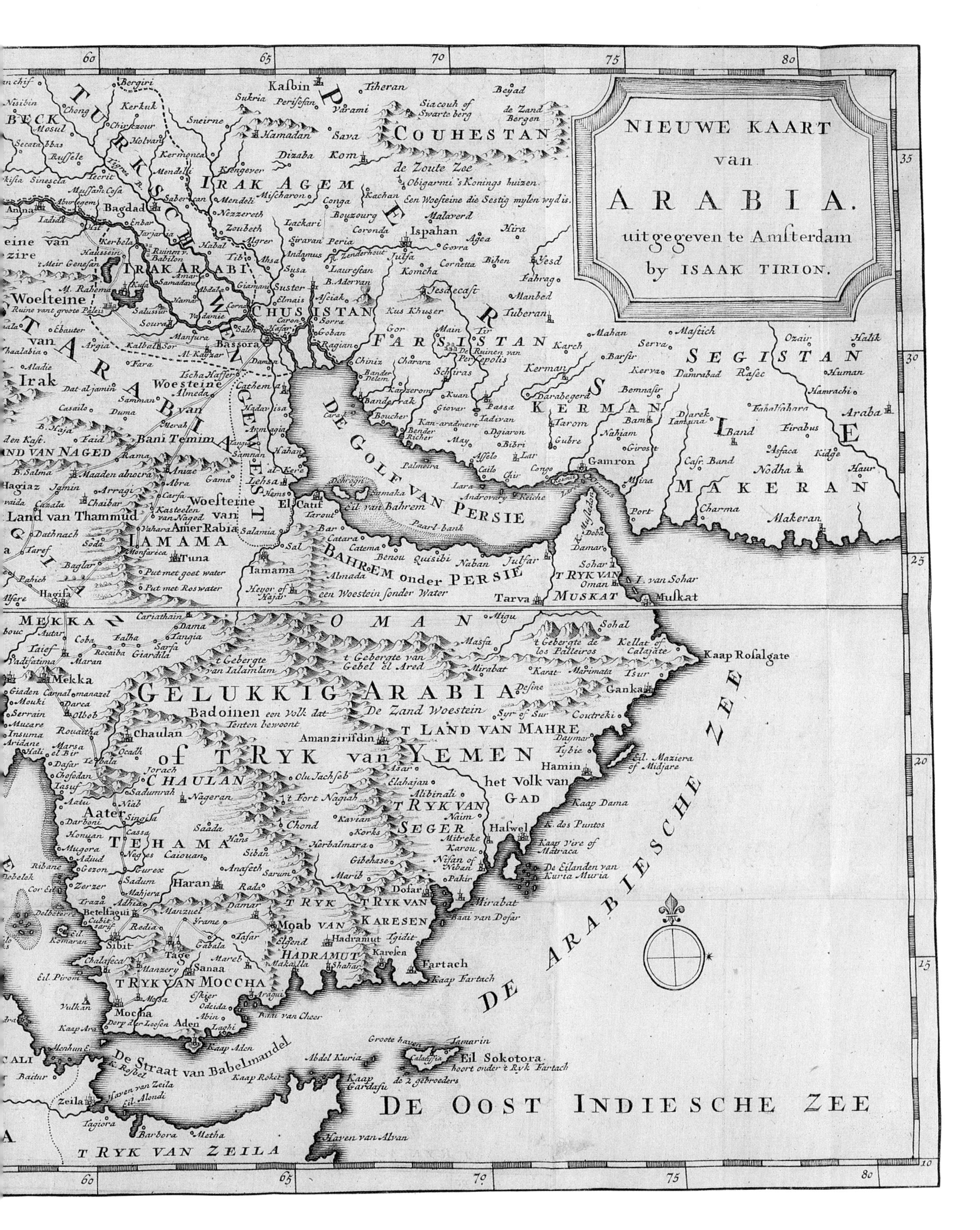
NIEUWE KAART
van
ARABIA.
uitgegeven te Amsterdam
by ISAAK TIRION.
60
65
70
75
80
35
30
25
20
15
10
TURKSCHE
IRAK AGEM
PERSIE
COUHESTAN
de Zoute Zee
Obigarmi 's Konings huizen.
Een Woesteine die Sestig mylen wydis.
Ispahan
Bagdad
IRAK ARABI
CHUSISTAN
FARSISTAN
SEGISTAN
KERMAN
Bassora
ARABIA
WESTGEWEST
Woesteine
DE GOLF VAN PERSIE
Eil. van Bahrem
Paarl-bank
BAHREM onder PERSIE
een Woestein sonder Water
Land van Thammud
IAMAMA
Put met goet water
Put met Roswater
Gamron
MAKERAN
T RYK VAN Oman
MUSKAT
Muskat
OMAN
Mekka
Kaap Rosalgate
GELUKKIG ARABIA
Badoinen een Volk dat Tenten bewoont
De Zand Woestein
T LAND VAN MAHRE
of T RYK van YEMEN
het Volk van GAD
T RYK VAN SEGER
CHAULAN
TEHAMA
Eil. Maziera of Midjare
Kaap Dama
De Eilanden van Kuria Muria
T RYK VAN KARESEN
HADRAMUT
Fartach
Kaap Fartach
T RYK VAN MOCCHA
Sanaa
Mocha
Aden
Kaap Aden
De Straat van Babelmandel
Eil Sokotora hoort onder t Ryk Fartach
Kaap Gardafu
DE ARABIESCHE ZEE
DE OOST INDIESCHE ZEE
T RYK VAN ZEILA
Zeila
Haven van Alvan

Plate 15 Detail of the map on plate 14.

Plate 16

The splendid map *Regnum Persicum, Imperium Turcicum in Asia Russorum Provinciae ad Mare Caspium* by the Ottens Brothers.
(Collection B.J. Slot [another copy in British Museum Maps 114.28])

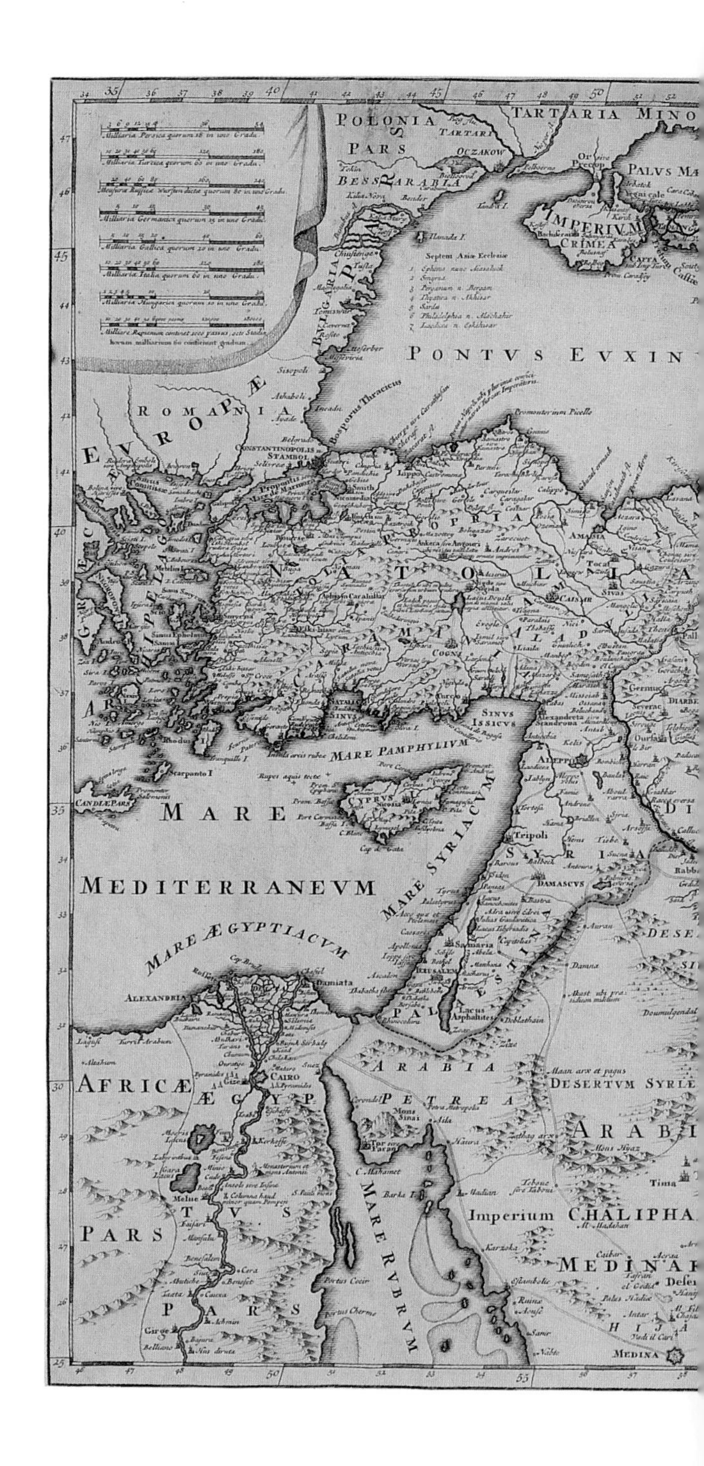

REGNUM PERSICUM
IMPERIUM TURCICUM in ASIA
RUSSORUM PROVINCIÆ ad MARE CASPIUM
aliæque regiones finitimæ,
item PONTI EUXINI, MARIS CASPII, ac SINUS PERSICI
novissimæ ac fidelissimæ delineationes
omnia ex variis observationibus
in lucem edita
a
REINERO et JOSUA OTTENS
Geographis Amstelædam.
RUSSIÆ MAGNÆ PARS
NAGAIA MAGNA
IEMBOLOVKI
CALMUCCI ALBI
COSACCI ERRANTES
ASTRACAN REGNUM
MARE CASPIUM
TARTARIA LIBERA
REGNUM USBECCORUM
REGNUM TACHKUNT
REGNUM CASCAR
TURQUESTAN
REGNUM MINORIS TIBET
CACHEMIR
REGNUM BALCH
CANDAHAR
CABOUL
INDI
SEGESTAN
SABLESTAN
ARROUCHAGE
REGNUM MOULTAN
MOGOLIS
MECRAN
ubi habitant Balluci sive Bullodges gens ferox et bellicosa
KIRMAN
LARESTAN
FARSISTAN
CHUSISTAN
IRACAGEMI
IRAC ARABI
ARMENIA
ERIVAN
SINUS PERSICUS
BAHREIN
REGNUM MASCATE
DESERTA
DESERTUM
NAJDA SEU NAGEDA
AMER RABIA
BANI TEMIM
REGIO DAHNÆ
SINUS GILAN
MASANDRAN
TABRISTIN
CORASAN
COUHESTAN
ASTRABAD
DEHESTAN
REGNUM CORCANG SEU CARIZMAE
TURCMENNI
GHIWIE
SINUS ASTRABAD
CHIRWAN
GEORGIA
CURDISTAN
ADERBIJANA
LAC. VAN

Corbeth
Lackari
Corrin
Consar
Deh Couchek
Dombi
Serehan
Malaverd
Abigerm
Caseni
Samagi
Nanui
Danarakié
Tchalisia
Corenda
Rie
Coopa
Agea
Sellef
Ardecan
al Chamare
Zoubeth
KAMALAVA
Jarjaria
Siravan
Turcomanni
PERIA
MASENDAN
ISPAHAN
Sabs
Golabad
Gaurume
Algrer
Kamalava
Armen
Habal sive Gabal
Zenderoud Fl.
Govra
Cornetta
Hemda
Godaña
Pahanar
GHANDEMAN
Caiac
Levicion
Laurestan
Ab Kuren fons
Biben seu Babain
Hazardara seu Mille-montes
Menil
Tib
Kercha
Susa
Jondisabur
LAVRESTAN
Komcha
Macs
Aron abad
Ocda
Manbed
Tom Zil
Je Ouaset
L. Ouaset
Mosenia
Escar mocran
Suster seu Tostar
M. Aderyan
Yesde cast
Giamani
Busodra
Aser
Boveiba
Ahouas
Mesercan
Asciac
Varm hormoz
Gombezcala
Dehi Gherdou
Jarcoia
GEZIRA
Sakie
Magrou
Etelent
Corna
Maber
CHVSISTAN
Kus Khuser
Gusti
ASTACH
Bend
Kehemend
el Rabaghia
Sahab
Caron
Sorra seu Dorac
Suc-sambil
Asoupas
Ardebil parva
Sivan
Soveib
Goban
Mnethel
Chemal
Argan
Ragian
Endian seu Tab Fl.
FARSISTAN
Rasain
Gor
Ilain
Tchilminar Reliquiæ
Persepolis
Tir
BASSORA
Goban
Endian
Horaidan
Korcheman
Abgherm
Vadigiad
Kelvan
Hobaian seu Zobaide
Campi
Planities Choadcheh
Cobrocia
Bassora vetus
Charara
Chalan
Zerca
Chiniz
Promont Domba
Bender Delem
Scheleston
Giovain
CHIRAS
Lacus Salsus
Gebel-Sinan M.
Daman
Tcha-Haffer
Buretum
Chadaghi
M. Anzira
Karzerom
Casra
Mouzeferia
Mamui
Ostia Tigris
Portus Cathemæ
I. Cargou
Bender Rik
Dris
Narghis
Sefid-rou
Naged
Paira
Kuan
Chafer
Jamengian
Passa
Almeda
Cathema
Hadavisa
I. Carac ab Arabibus culta
Coucher
Corsiara
Boucher
Tadivan
Giovar
Mouchek
Nesirbad
Armagia
Hahan
Putei
Tangia
Bender Richer
Dast
Surab
Dgiaron
Firuzabad
Giar
Kan-ara
Tchaitel
Dehi Dombe
Benaru
Montquelai
Congon
Kabrend
Samnan
al-Kere
Prom. Verdostan
Gallus pulvinus periculosus
I. Palmeira
Chetlo
May
Asselo
Naban
DESERTVM
Ghama
Meslehan
SINVS PERSICVS
Sinus Estornardy
Cailo
Portus Catif
Dehrogn
Samaka
I. Lara
I. Androvary sive dos Paxaros
Alahsa sive Lehsa
Aniza
Hems
Catif
AMER RABIA
Merab
Tarout
Insula Bahrein
Pulvinus Bahrein ubi Margaritæ leguntur jussu Persarum Regis
Naid seu Naged
Putei
Hagiar
Borani
Biscia
GEDA
BAHREIN

Plate 17

Part of the map on plate 16: the Gulf area.

Maber
Varm hormoz
CHVSISTAN
Etelent
Corna
Nehrovan
Sahab
Caron
Sorra seu Dorac
Kerri
Morra
Addir
Soveib
Goban
Suc-sambil
Hafar
Mnethel
Argan
Batsec Sirin
Makel
BASSORA
Regmla
Chemal
Ragian
Obolla
Cobrocia
Bassora vetus
Goban
Endian
Jeoudi
Ab-Kassir
Emir
Chader
Madian
Dorges
Chiniz
Promont Domba
Ostia Tigris
Daman
Buretum
Portus Cathemæ
Bender Rik
I. Cargou
Cathema
Hadavisa
I. Carac ab Arabibus culta
SINVS
Armagia
Hahan
al-Kere
Samnan
Gallus

Plate 18

Cathema (Kazima), detail of the map on plate 16.

The brothers Reynier and Josua Ottens were map-makers who specialized in large-size maps out of which they compiled custom-made atlases for very rich clients. Their map of the Ottoman Empire and Persia is a very fine example of their work. The map bears no date, but it was advertised for sale in 1737.[15] It is an up-to-date compilation of geographic knowledge available at that time. Like Tirion's map it has clear borderlines around Ottoman Iraq, and Cathema is located outside Iraq. A new feature is that it has Aguada Island in front of Cathemae. Rather interesting is the mention of Portus Cathemae (harbour of Kazima) as a geographical name on the map. This could indicate the Gulf of Kuwait although no inlet is shown on this map.

The curvy line between the 'h' and the 'e' in the name Cathema is the legendary Bahrain river between Bahrain and Basra.

15 Van der Krogt, *Advertenties*, p. 147.

Plate 19

The maps of the German publisher J.B. Homann had a very wide circulation. This map of 1737 shows Cathema in the style of Tirion.
(General State Archives of The Netherlands, Maps and Drawings Department TOPO 16 A 217A)

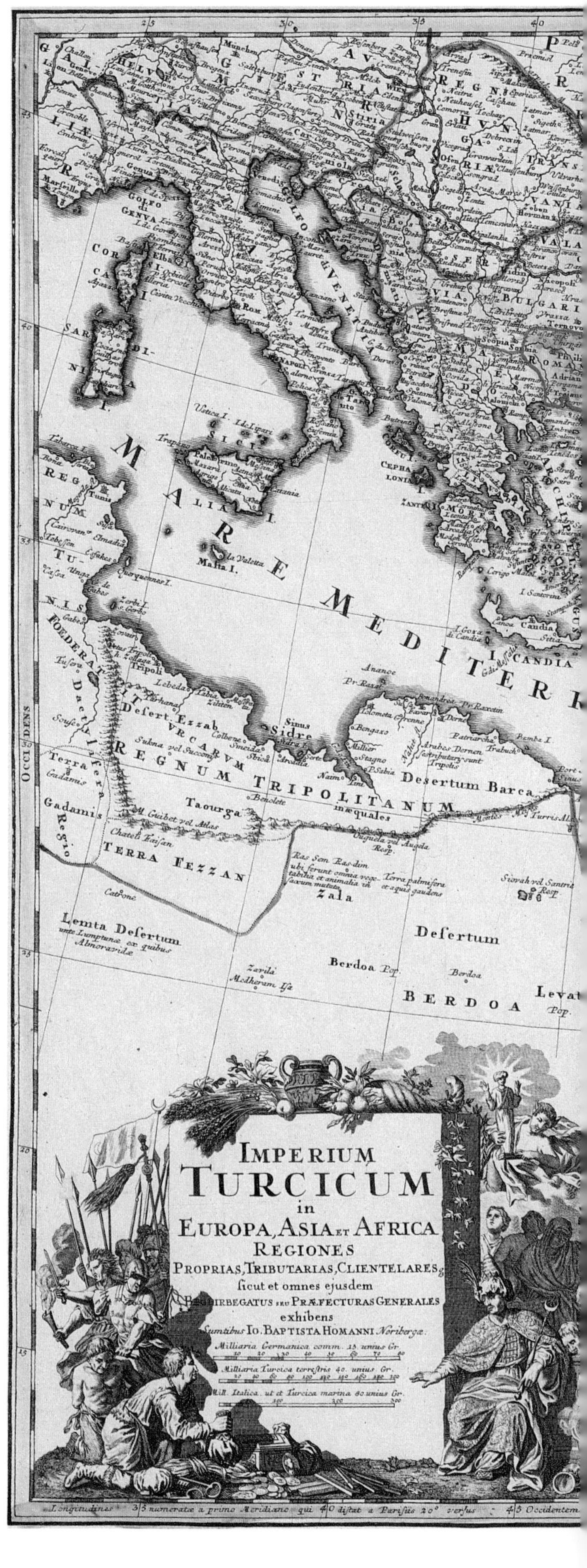

Plate 20

Detail of the map on plate 19.

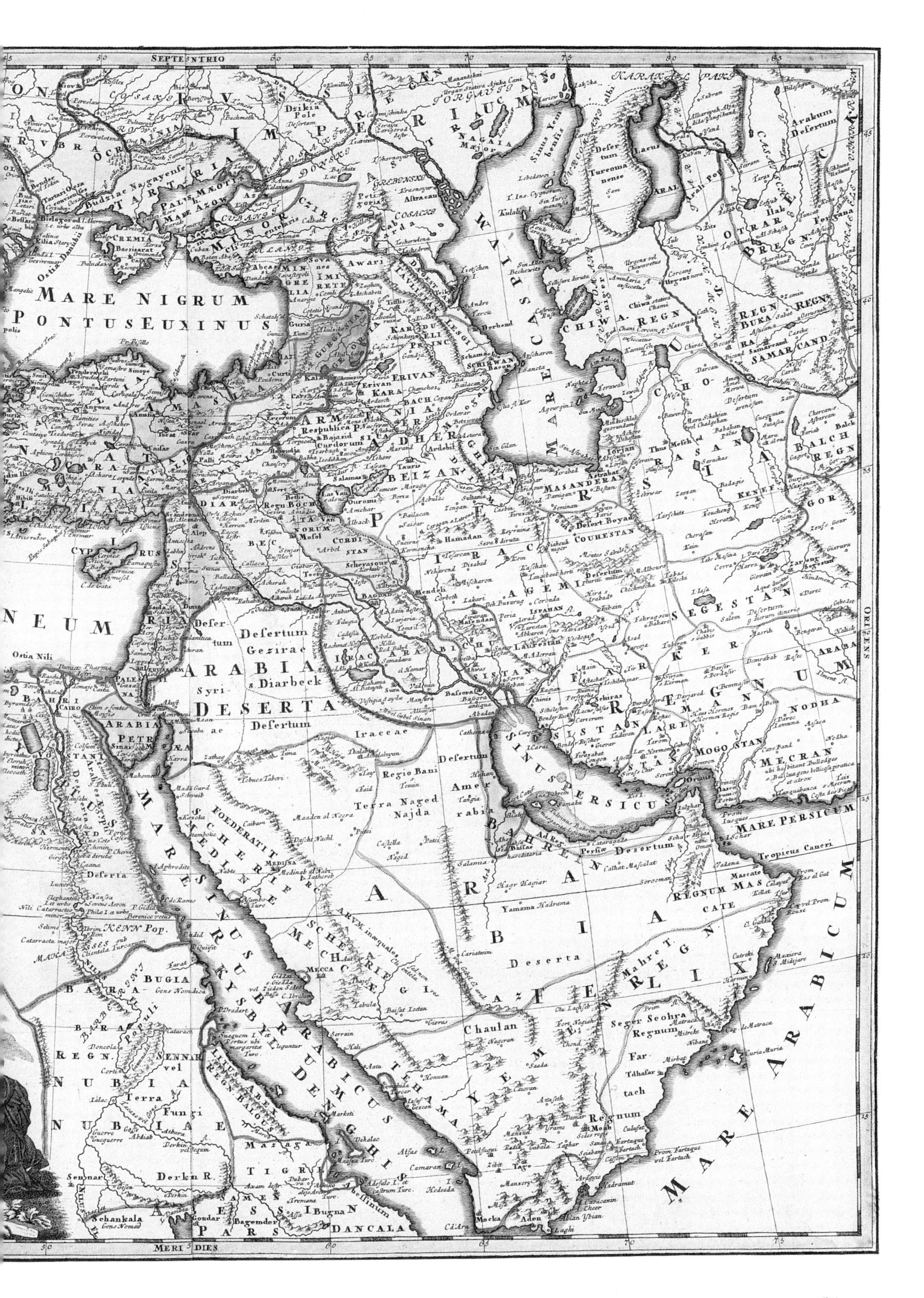
SEPTENTRIO
MERIDIES
ORIENS
MARE NIGRUM
PONTUS EUXINUS
MARE CASPIUM
ARABIA DESERTA
SINUS PERSICUS
MARE PERSICUM
MARE ARABICUM
ARABIA FELIX
SINUS ARABICUS
MARE RUBRUM
Tropicus Cancri

Part 3
AGUADA BECOMES FAYLAKA

In the course of the eighteenth century, the Portuguese name Ilha de Aguada was replaced on some maps and nautical charts with Peluche, a version of the Arab name Faylaka which approaches the local pronunciation of the name.
Some later maps show Faylaka in front of Kazima.

The Portuguese had given the island of Faylaka, situated off the entrance of the Gulf of Kuwait, the name of Ilha de Aguada, island of the waterwell. The name was appropriate: Faylaka has water. After 1730 Aguada is called Peluche on some maps, reflecting the local pronunciation Feltsha. Probably the oldest version is to be found on one of the three maps of the Gulf bound in a manuscript atlas of the Dutch East Indies by Liébault, made in the years 1728-1740 and to be found among the collection of the Service Historique de la Marine in Brest in France. The next mention of the name Peluche is on the nautical chart of the coasts of the Arabian peninsula in the French nautical atlas *Neptune Oriental* of 1740, which was reproduced in an edition by Prévost in 1745.[16] Both the Liébault atlas and the Prévost map lean heavily on Dutch nautical maps, either on unknown manuscripts or on the version published in London by Thornton. It is not certain, however, whether the appearance of the name Peluche originates from French observations or from a Dutch manuscript which has not been unearthed, but was a source to Liébault's atlas of the Dutch East Indies.

[16] *Neptune Oriental* (Paris 1740). A.F. Prévost *Histoire générale des voyages*, vol. 1 (Paris 1745).

Plate 21 Detail of the chart of the *Neptune Oriental* of 1740. According to its vignette, it is based on observations by the Captain of the French East India Company le Floch de la Carrière, but these observations did not extend to the area of Kuwait. Its drawing of the rivers below Basra is rather inaccurate when compared with the much older manuscript by Roobacker of 1645 (plate 3) or De Haan's copy of a Dutch manuscript contemporary to the *Neptune Oriental* (plate 23).
(Collection Dr. Sultan bin Muhammad Al-Qasimi)

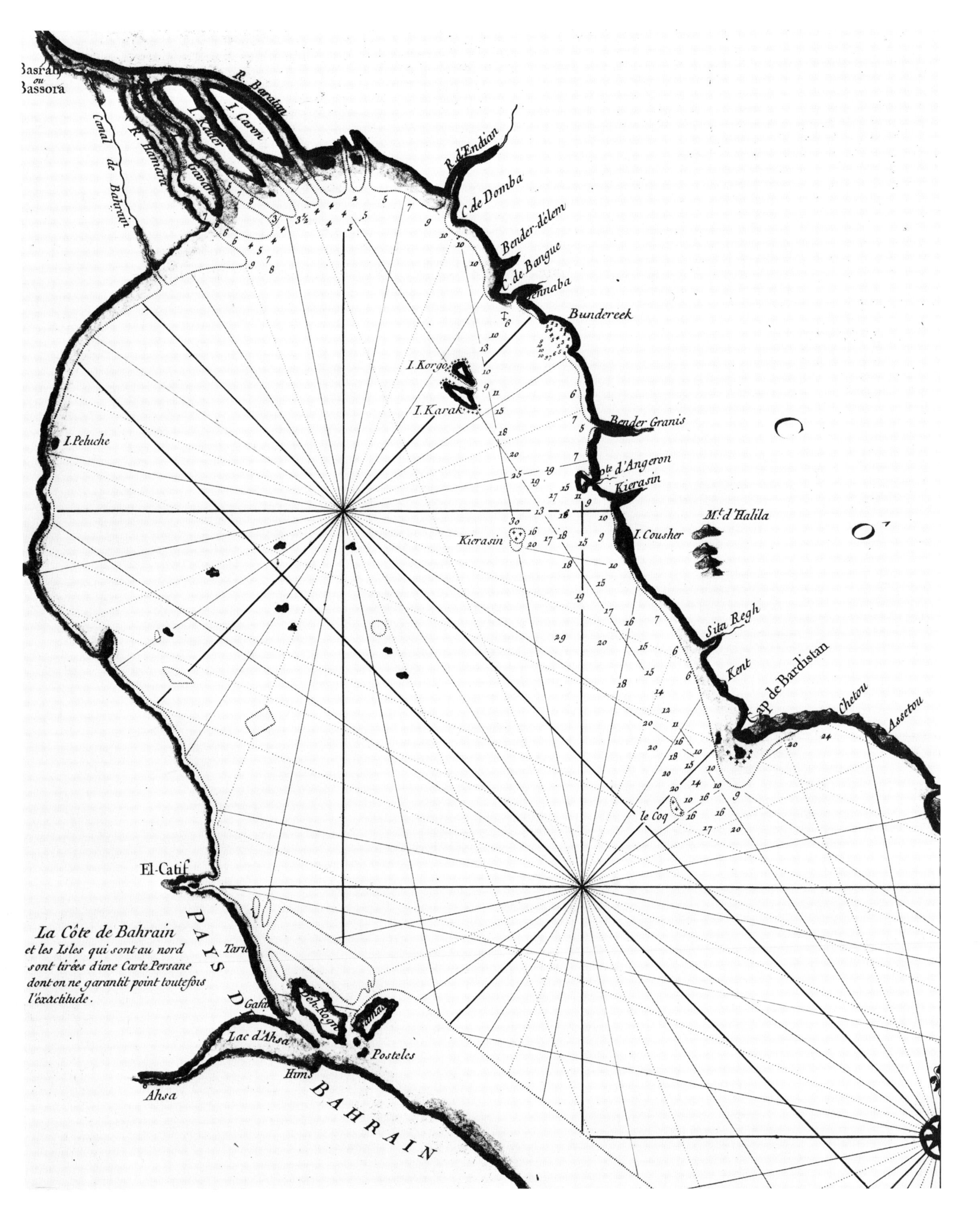
Basrah ou Bassora
I. Caron
Canal de Bahrain
R. d'Endian
C. de Domba
Bender-délem
C. de Bangue
Bundereek
I. Korgo
I. Karak
Bender Granis
I. Peluche
Pte d'Angeron
Kierasin
Mt d'Halila
I. Cousher
Kierasin
Sita Regh
Kent
Cap de Bardistan
Chetou
Assetou
le Coq
El-Catif
PAYS D
BAHRAIN
Lac d'Ahsa
Posteles
Ahsa
La Côte de Bahrain
et les Isles qui sont au nord
sont tirées d'une Carte Persane
dont on ne garantit point toutefois
l'exactitude.

Plate 22

The map published by Prévost in 1745 is one of the first printed maps to have the name of Peluche. It had a very wide circulation.
(Library of the General State Archives of The Netherlands)

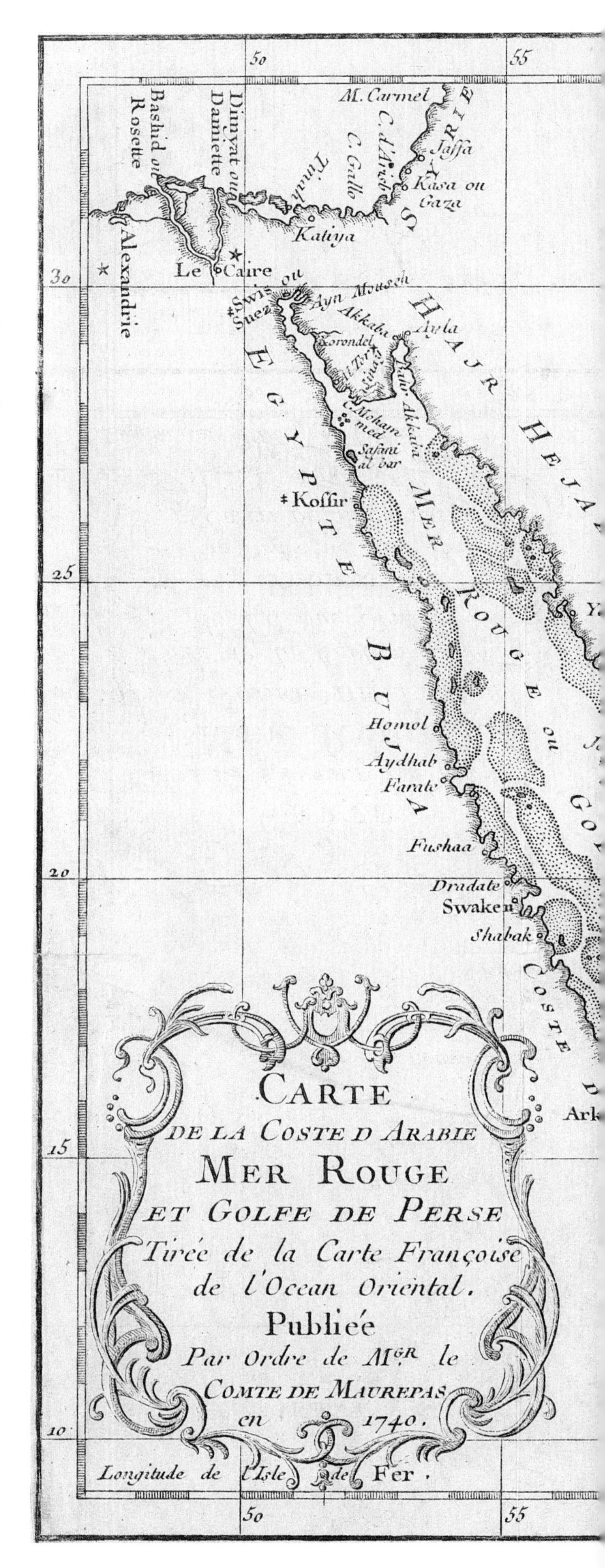

Nota.
★ Lieux où il y a observations astronomiques de Latitude et de Longitude.
‡ Observations astronom. de Latitude.
‡ Observations de Latitude faites par d'habiles Navigateurs.
IRAK
Hellah
Korna
Ahwaz
Sura
Basrah
Endian
Bandar Dilem
Bandar Rik
Kargo
Karak
I. Peleche
Zesarin
C. Rokte
Bandar Risher
Angera
C. Verdiston
Chetton
R. Nabon
R. Darabin
Bandar Kongo
Gomrun ou Bandar Abbasi
I. Monjela
C. Nabon
I. Lara
Bahrayn
Al Katif
Pearl Bank
Katara
Goda
BAHRAYN
Julfar
Detroit d'Ormus
Jaskes
R. Ipsrum
C. Jaskes
Daba
Longrissoa
Habor
Hunnok
Varak
Swada
Maskat
Kuriat
Zoar
Ras algat
C. Kuriat
C. Kalayat
MASKAT
Kanara
Spallura
S. Peters B.
I. Maziera ou Mijara
Malriaka
C. Isoletta
Matakna
Matkoa
C. S. Pedro
I. Chartan et Martan ou Kuria Muria
Merbat
Dhofar
Sajar
Watering Place
Harwel
C. Fartak
Sanaa ou Zenan
Kushem ou Kashin
Sharnin Pt
Rider
C. Boagashowa
Makulla
Argel
Zabid
Kamaran I.
Mokha
Aden
C. Aden
Moeras
I. Prin
Belula
Assab
Bahayta
Mt al Mondul
Babalmandel
Zeyla
Jajoura
Barbora
I. Demiti
Feluk
C. Guar da Fui
Delli Shah
Tamarin
I. Sokotra
Duas Hermanas ou les deux Sœurs
I. Abdal Kuria
C. Dorfui ou del Goada
Baba Feluk ou Mt Felix
R. S. Peter
ARABIE
YAMAN
TAHAMAH
MEKKE
la Meke
ZEYLA
ou ADEL
Detroit ou de Babalmandel
60
65
70
75
30
25
20
15
10

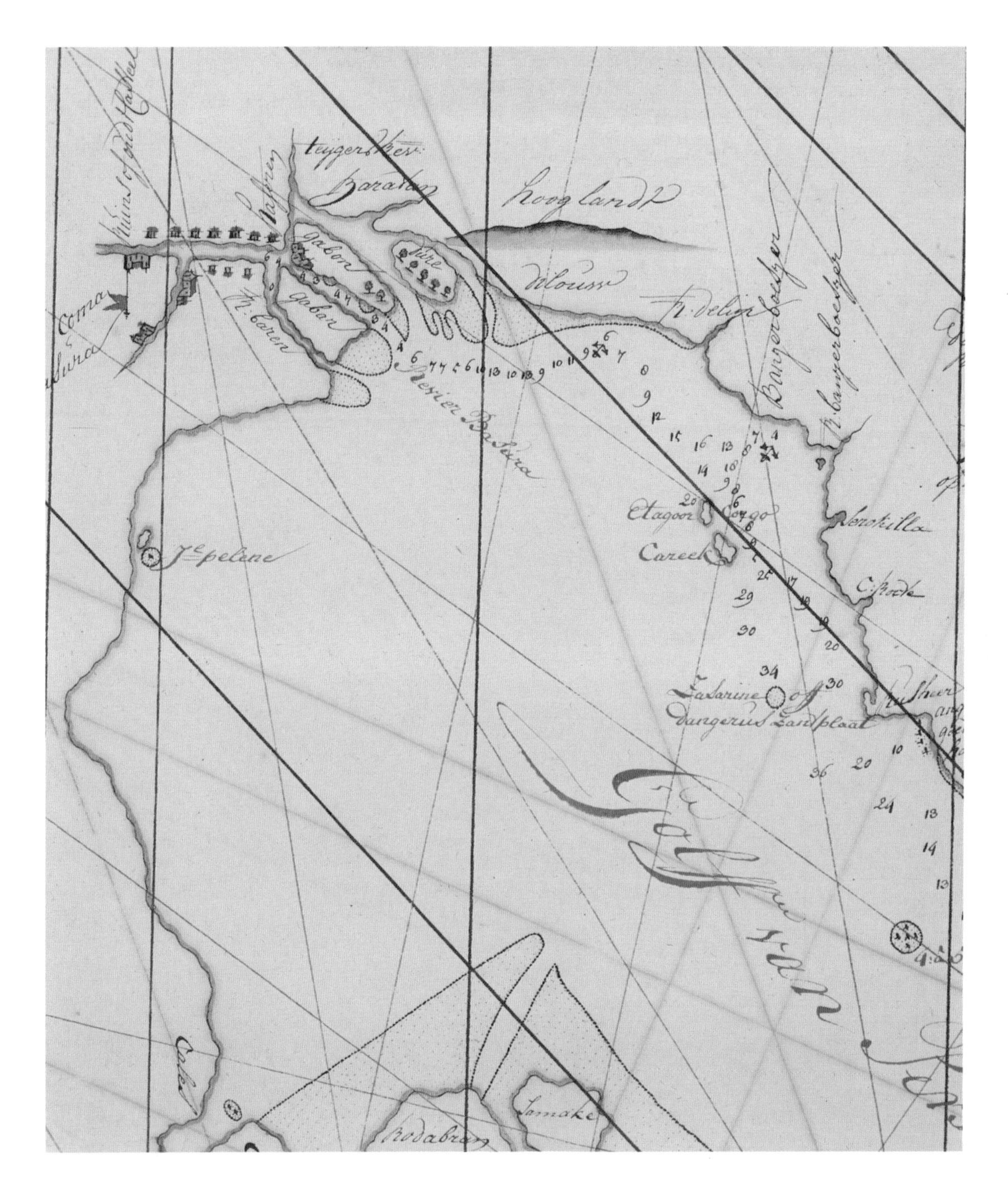

Plate 23 Part of a large manuscript chart of the Gulf by Gerrit de Haan from his atlas of the Dutch East India Company of 1760. It also bears the name Peluche for Faylaka. This chart seems to be derived from an unknown Dutch manuscript chart which served as a source to Liébault.
(General State Archives of The Netherlands, Maps and Drawings Department VELH 156, vol. 2, chart no. 14)

Plate 24 Part of J. Bourguignon d'Anville's map of Arabia of 1755; this is the first map combining Kazima and Faylaka.
(Leiden University Library)

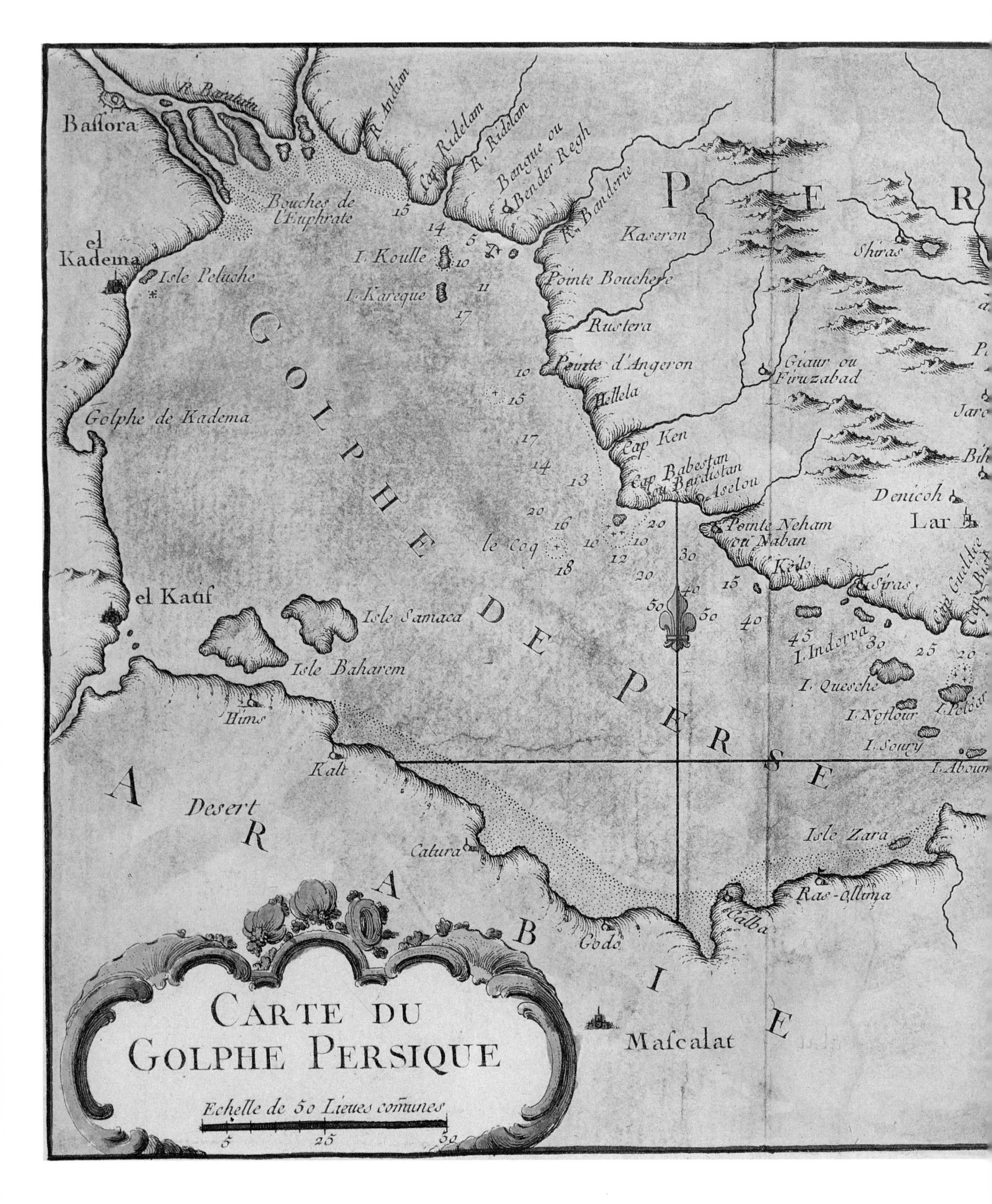
Carte du Golphe Persique
Echelle de 50 Lieues comunes
Golphe de Perse
Bassora
Bouches de l'Euphrate
el Kadema
Isle Peluche
I. Koulle
I. Kareque
Golphe de Kadema
el Katif
Isle Samaca
Isle Baharem
Arabie
Desert
Kalt
Catura
Godo
Mascalat
Calba
Ras-ollima
Isle Zara
Kaseron
Pointe Bouchere
Rustera
Pointe d'Angeron
Hellela
Cap Ken
Giaur ou Firuzabad
Shiras
Denicoh
Lar
Pointe Neham ou Naban
I. Indorva
I. Quesche
I. Neflour
I. Soury
le Coq

Plate 25

The French cartographer Bonne published a great many maps. He certainly was not the most advanced map-maker of his time, but the maps he published of the Gulf between the years 1760 and 1780 show an interesting mixture of two older traditions in map-making. In the area of Kuwait he copies the combination of Kazima and Faylaka already found in D'Anville.
(Collection Dr. Sultan bin Muhammad Al-Qasimi)

Part 4
GRAIN AND THE UTUB

During the first half of the eighteenth century, first mention is made of the Utub, the Arab tribe which played an essential part in Kuwait becoming a state.
During this period, the place of Grain, the name of Utub Kuwait in the earliest European sources, seems to have grown in significance. In 1750 it was already a centre of considerable importance.
The orthography of the name of Grain (phonetically speaking, a more correct transcription would be Qrayn) in the European sources shows an astonishing variety: Green, Grijn, Graine, Grane, Grän.

First mentions of the Utub tribe

The origins and early history of the Utub tribe remains very vague. Local tradition, as related in Abu-Hakima's books and by some older Kuwaiti historians, is that this tribe was a branch of the great Anaza tribe which started to migrate in the second half of the seventeenth century under the protection of the powerful Banu Khalid tribe which dominated the area between Al Hasa and Iraq. There are several different stories. The Utub first went to the area of Qatar. Later, according to one tradition, they lived in Basra for some time or, according to another tradition, in Southern Persia. Finally, they migrated to the area of Kuwait.[17]

The accuracy of these Kuwaiti local traditions is confirmed by an Ottoman document dating back to 1701, which has been available for some time, but has not been correctly interpreted until now. It was published in facsimile, with an Arab translation and an English translation in the Bahraini historical periodical *Al Watheeka* by A. Aba Hussain.[18]

The document is a formal report (*ilâm*) by Ali, the recently appointed Pasha of Basra, to the Ottoman central government. The Pasha states that once in the area of Bahrain, dominated by *'adjam* ('non-Arab speakers'), had lived the Utub and Khalifat tribes. In the English translation in *Al Watheeka* the word *'adjam* is translated as Europeans. This would be a quite acceptable translation, were it not that the Europeans were not in Bahrain at this time. The island was under Persian influence until it was conquered by Omani forces in 1717. In this text *'adjam* seems to be a rather unfriendly word used by the Ottomans for the Persians. We would also propose a different interpretation of the word Khalifat than the one used in *Al Watheeka*. Instead of reading it as Al Khalifa, which would be attractive, but makes a tribe out of a family, we propose to keep to the text as it is written in the Ottoman document. The Khalifat was an Arab tribe living in the area of Bandar Daylam in Southern Persia; in this document it is also mentioned in connection with Bandar Daylam.[19] This different interpretation makes the Ottoman document an interesting confirmation of existing traditions among the Utub in Kuwait.
The document states that the Utub and the Khalifat were chased away from the area of Bahrain by the Huwala, who lived in Bandar Kong (near the actual Bandar Lengeh) and Bandar Ferayhin (in Qatar), in collusion with the *'adjam*. The Utub and the Khalifat hit back, plundering Bahrain and killing many of the Huwala. Then they became frightened

[17] Abu Hakima, *Modern History of Kuwait*, p. 4.

[18] A. Aba Hussain, 'A Study of the History of Utoob', *Al Watheeka* 1 (1982), pp. 25–42; Arab version on pp. 94–107, a facsimile of the document on p. 102, the Arab translation on p. 102 and the English translation on p. 39.

[19] Description of the Khalifat in a report of 1756 in General State Archives of The Netherlands, Aanwinsten Eerste Afdeling 1889 23B, fols. 9–9v.

of reprisals and many migrated to Basra, where they occupied 2000 houses. They were quite a powerful group, owning 150 ships armed with some light artillery, which they used for merchant shipping, and for transporting goods for Basra merchants. It is not yet clear what their final plans were, but Ali Pasha thought of offering them a permanent abode in Basra. Ali Pasha's motives for this offer are not difficult to imagine. The trade of the tribesmen would increase the customs revenues, and consequently would increase his own income. It is possible that the Pasha exaggerated the military power of the tribesmen in order to show the central authorities that the establishment of these tribesmen might improve the difficult strategic position of Basra.

It is most gratifying that this document in the Ottoman archives confirms the Utub's traditions relating that they had come through Basra or Southern Iran: both traditions are true.

For the general understanding of this important document, it is useful to place it in the context of its regional history. It is known that shortly before 1674, a coalition of Arab tribes in the area between Basra and Bandar Rig (this area includes the land of the Khalifat) had chased the Huwala from the pearlbanks of Bahrain.[20] The Ottoman document implies that, at a certain unknown moment, the Huwala of the Lower Gulf had regained control, but that the Utub and the Khalifat had taken bloody revenge for their losses. They had come to fear reprisals and had turned to Basra. They went there at a rather difficult moment in Basra's history. For a short time it had been under Persian rule, but after concluding peace with Austria and Venice in 1698, the Ottoman Empire had been able to restore its authority over the town of Basra in 1701 (but not over much of the surrounding territory). We might even question whether the Utub had established themselves in the town when it was under Persian rule. Ottoman rule in the area was subject to the constant threat of attack from the Muntafiq Arabs. In that same year 1701, the Utub arrived requesting to stay. Ali, a tyrant according to reports of the Dutch East India Company, was Pasha of Basra until 1705 when he was replaced by Khamis Pasha. In the meantime, the town had been devastated by the plague in 1704 and was plundered by the Muntafiq Arabs in 1706.

Apparently, no action was taken on Ali Pasha's report. If there had been any result, one would have expected at least some later reference to the affair in the Mühimme registers in the Ottoman archives. There is no further mention of the Khalifat or the Utub as residents of Basra. The Khalifat must have moved back to Bandar Daylam. According to their own tradition, the Utub were chased from Basra by the Ottoman Government because they were a hindrance to shipping in the Shatt al Arab. Somehow, and at some point in time, they arrived in Kuwait, several days of travel away from Basra and in an area which was completely outside the control of the Basra Government. This region was under the control of the Banu Khalid, who were not particularly friendly with the

[20] Carré, *Travels*, vol. 1, p. 101; vol. 3, pp. 827–830.

Ottomans. A very late English source, probably based on oral tradition in Kuwait, puts the date of this settlement at 1716. There is no real proof that this tradition is accurate, but it fits in well with the general history of the Gulf. The period 1715-1717 was a period of great turmoil in the Gulf. From October 1715 onwards, the Omanis made several attempts to conquer Bahrain from the Persians. Trade at Basra was almost at a standstill.[21] Migration away from Basra would not be unexpected in such circumstances.
After this, there are no known direct references to the Utub for almost 40 years. The next mention of the Utub occurs in a crucial period for the Arab tribes who lived around the Gulf. This was during the short period when Persia's military power underwent a revival under Nadir Shah, who tried to conquer Ottoman Iraq.
For this he needed a navy, and he obtained one by buying European ships and manning them with Arab tribesmen from the shores of the Gulf. The navy was first put to the test in May 1736 when they conquered Bahrain from the Huwala tribesmen who had possessed that island for some time. Next year the Persian navy was used to intervene in the chronic Omani civil war. These operations were not successful and several Arab tribes along the Persian coast no longer submitted to Persian authority. In the course of 1738, the Banu Khalid allied with the Huwala (a most unusual coalition of traditional enemies), in an attack on Bahrain. The attack failed, but hostilities between the Banu Khalid and the Persians continued. Nadir Shah was unable to inspire the Huwala tribesmen who manned much of his navy with loyalty. In 1740 a great mutiny and a general rebellion among the Huwala broke out, and in this context the Utub are mentioned as allies of the Huwala.
This mention of the Utub by the French consul in Basra, Jean Otter, is the first mention of this tribe in a Western source. Little more than the name of the tribe is mentioned; there is no mention of the place where they are based.[22]
Otter's text is as follows:

...The Hula and the Bani Utba Arabs revolted against Thamas Khan [=Nadir Shah]. By his order, several of their boats had been taken for a secret expedition and seven ships had been prepared for the same purpose. Mir Ali Khan, who commanded this fleet, had treated the Arabs rather badly. They killed him, captured some of his ships and left...

[21] *Generale Missiven*, vol. 7, pp. 253, 317, 440; General State Archives of the Netherlands, Archives of the Dutch East India Company vol. 1886, fols. 95, 137–138, 169.
[22] They are mentioned in Otter's private notes in the Bibliothèque Nationale, Paris, Fonds Français no. 989, fol. 71. The notes are also in Otter's *Voyage*, p. 130.

Grain

The early history of the Utub in Grain is a very confused one. The first direct mention of their presence there is in a Dutch document of 1756, but by that time they had already very much settled there. Grain is mentioned in Dutch sources as an established centre of trade in 1750. The source material used in writing the history of Kuwait concerning the period before 1750 does not look very reliable. There are local traditions, written down long years after the events, and reports by British colonial officials based on hearsay in 1814 or later.

The best sources seem to be the Kuwaiti traditions stating that Kuwait originated sometime in the seventeenth century as a village, slowly growing in size near a summer residence of the Banu Khalid, possibly in the area of Jahra at the upper end of the Gulf of Kuwait. This looks like another side of the history of Kazima as indicated by the European maps. According to the same local traditions, the Utub arrived early in the eighteenth century, after the adventures recorded in the Ottoman document of 1701. No certainty exists about the details of dynastic history recorded in the British reports of the early nineteenth century. After having left Basra, the Utub had to look for a new dwelling, which they found in Kuwait. It is impossible to put a date to this event. It must have been some time before 1750 because Grain was already well established in that year, but it remains impossible to be more specific.

The first mentions of Grain in European documents are connected with a great scandal in the Dutch East India Company. A certain Frans Canter, a Roman Catholic and citizen of the town of Amsterdam, had been Principal Resident of the establishment of the Company since 1747. In 1749, the Governor General of the Dutch East Indies wanted to replace him with Baron Tiddo Frederik van Kniphausen. Hearing of the arrival of Kniphausen, Canter, who seems to have been guilty of embezzling, fled beyond the reach of Basra, to Grain. From there, he joined a caravan which was going on a direct journey from Grain to Aleppo. From the port of Iskenderun, near Aleppo, Canter travelled to Amsterdam, where the East India Company was unable to get him prosecuted by the autonomous government of this town.

Canter's flight to Grain is a typical manifestation of a basic characteristic of Kuwait. Its essential function in the life of the Gulf at that time was that it was an area outside the sphere of influence of the Ottoman Government of Basra. In this way, it could serve as a refuge for both persons and trade when, for one reason or another, there was risk of trouble in Basra. This little desert trading town was born and continued to grow because of the simple fact of its being outside the troubled area of Ottoman Iraq.

During his stay in Grain, Canter wrote a letter which is the oldest surviving letter written in Kuwait. The original of the letter has not been found, but in the course of legal proceedings an authenticated abstract was made by an Amsterdam notary, which is now in the General State Archives.

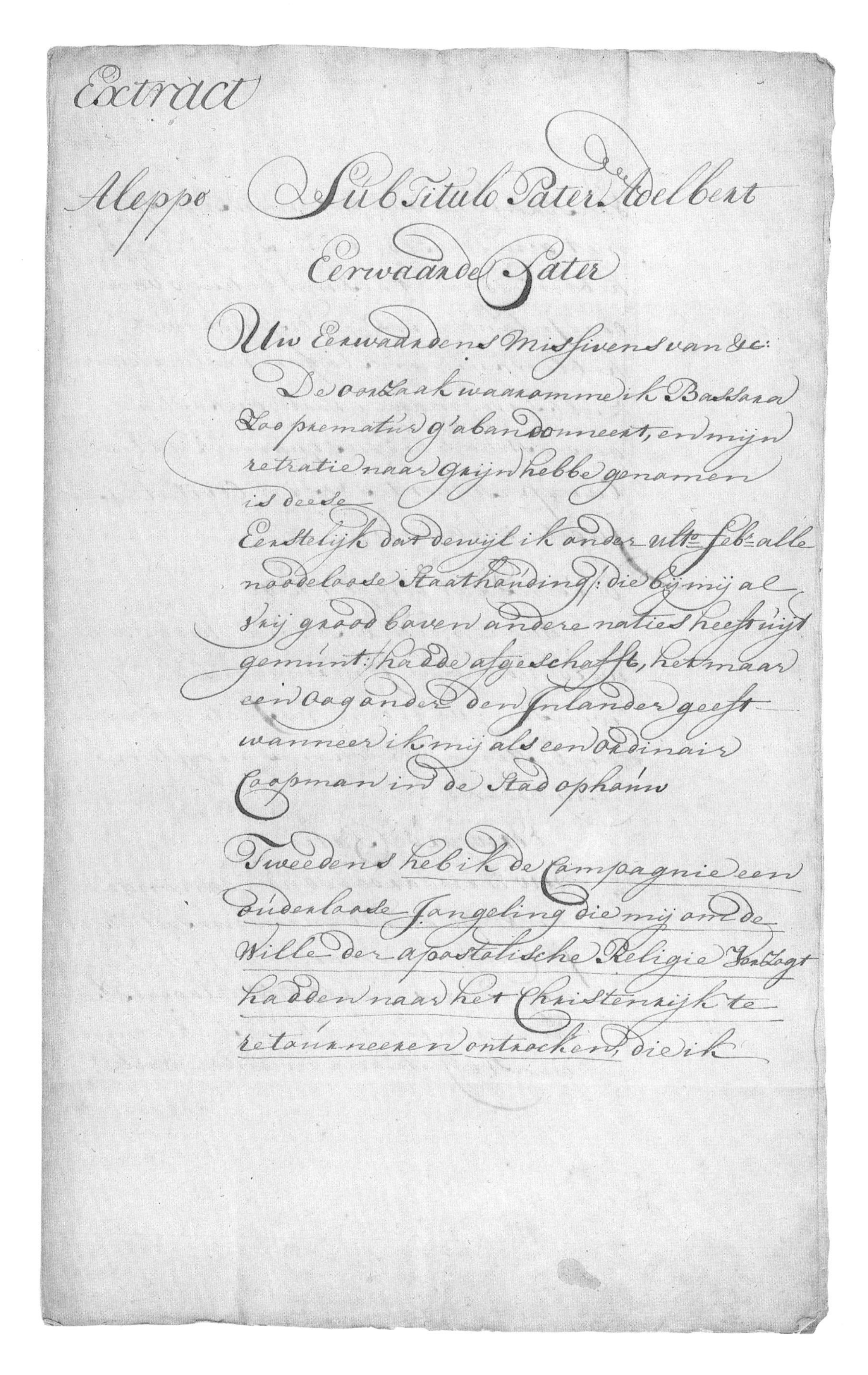

Extract

Aleppo. Sub Titulo Pater Adelbert

Eerwaarde Pater

Uw Eerwaardens Missiven van &c:

De oorzaak waaromme ik Bassora
zoo prematuur g'abandonneert, en mijn
retratie naar Grijn hebbe genomen
is deese

Eerstelijk dat dewijl ik onder ult° feb:° alle
noodelooze staathanding: die bij mij al
zeij groot boven andere naties heeft uijt
gemunt; hadde afgeschafft, het maar
een oog ander den Inlander geeft
wanneer ik mij als een ordinair
Coopman in de Stad ophauw

Tweedens heb ik de Campagnie een
ondenlaode Jangeling die mij om de
Wille der apostolische Religie verzagt
hadden naar het Christenrijk te
retourneeren ontrocken, die ik

Plate 26 Page from Frans Canter's letter written in Kuwait.
(General State Archives of The Netherlands, Aanwinsten Eerste Afdeling 1935 v 48)

Translation of the letter written in Grain on plate 26.

Addressed to Father Adelbert in Aleppo

Reverend Father
Your letter of etc.[23]
The reason why I left Basra prematurely and retreated to Grijn [Grain] is the following. Firstly, because I stopped all unnecessary ceremonial, which put me in status high above the merchants of other nations. Among the locals it would cause astonishment if I stayed in the town as a private merchant.
Secondly, because I took from the authority of the Company one young man who, for love of the Catholic religion, had asked me to be brought back to Christian Europe, and I had understood that my successor planned to bring him under his power by force. He could only have executed his plan with the support of the local authorities, and this would only have caused large expenses so I considered that
Third, because I etc.
I will end this letter by telling you of my high esteem for your person after having wished you perfect health and continuing strength.
Reverend Father
Your devout and obliged servant
(signed) F. Canter

In the village of Grijn [Grain], March 4 1750

[23] The abstract was shortened by the notary at some points.

There are some more letters referring to Canter's flight from Basra to Kuwait. The Dutch Ambassador in Istanbul was informed of it by a functionary of the Dutch consulate in Syria, Pollard, who reported from Aleppo on May 4, 1750 in Italian:

... and to give you the confirmed news that Mr Canter has fled from Basra the night of the 8th of March (old calendar) without rendering account of the money and merchandise to his successor. They say that he stays in an Arab village called Grain with the intention of coming to Aleppo on the earliest occasion...[24]

A few more of the many documents on Canter's flight contain references to Grain. The document on the following pages is of special interest because it shows that in 1750 Grain had direct caravan traffic with Syria, without a connecting route with Basra. This also implies that the port of Grain must already have been of such importance that it was worthwhile for caravans to come just to Grain, and this indicates that Grain had already been in existence for a number of years.

[24] General State Archives of The Netherlands, Archives of the embassy in Turkey prior to 1811, no. 382.

d'impegnarsi fortamte in favor del soggetto, unendosi con
il nostro Ambasciatore per rimediare subitamte questo
affronto con castigare l'autore di simil tumulto, che anno
messo in confusione e risico tutti li Effetti dei Franchi
e loro Privilegii in questa Piazza, e liberare il detto
Innocente dalla man dei Tiranni. Mi trovo in tal stato
per mancanza del mio Dragomano che non posso esseguire
alcuna cosa in favore dei Sigri Mercanti o altre Protetti
e questo cattivo atto della Porta senza dubio causara un
grand Danno per tutti. La causa di questo Commando
era per aver cercato fortemte di ricuperare il Danno di
ƒ.40,000 che ha sofferto da Mahmet Pasha il quale aveva
pigliato le sue Mercanzie per forsa dalla Dogana in
Bagdat. Per maggior ampla sua notitia li prego d'in-
formarsi dal nostro Ambasciatore come per l'angustia e
mancanza di tempo non posso piu stendermi. Mi trovo
sempre pronto a suoi ordini, rassegnandomi d'esser,

Di sua Eccelenza,

Humilmo Devotmo
ed obligatmo Servre
Ar: Pollard

P.S. li 27. del Corrte
parti un grand Caravana
per Bassora, con che fu spedita
Cocineglia in molto abondanza
destinata per la Persia, andara per
via di Grain senza attaccarsi a Bassora.

Sua Eccelza Elbert Barone di Hochepied.

Plate 27 Page of Pollard's letter in Aleppo, June 1st 1750, giving news of Canter's flight. On this page the postscript about caravan movements between Grain and Syria. (General State Archives of The Netherlands, Archives of the embassy in Turkey prior to 1811, no. 382)

Text of the relevant parts of the document on plate 27

...The last news I had about Mr. Giacomo [sic] Canter is that he was in the town of Grain, situated on the river Tigris, with the intention of travelling together with the caravan which is expected to arrive in about three weeks time in Aleppo. Our consul has written to me that Canter has left Basra in secret without clearing his account with his successor Baron Kniphausen. He has also taken away with him a large sum of money...
P.S. The 27th of this month, a large caravan left from here for Basra. With it was sent a very large quantity of cochenilla for Persia. But this caravan will go by way of Grain without passing Basra.

Canter's successor Kniphausen also notified his superiors, the Governor General and Council of the Dutch East Indies, of Canter's flight, though in his official report of August 10, 1750 he has only a short mention of it.

...The resident Canter who has deserted has taken his way from Green through the desert to Aleppo...[25]

[25] General State Archives of The Netherlands, Archives of the Dutch East India Company vol. 2787, section Basra, pp. 24–25.

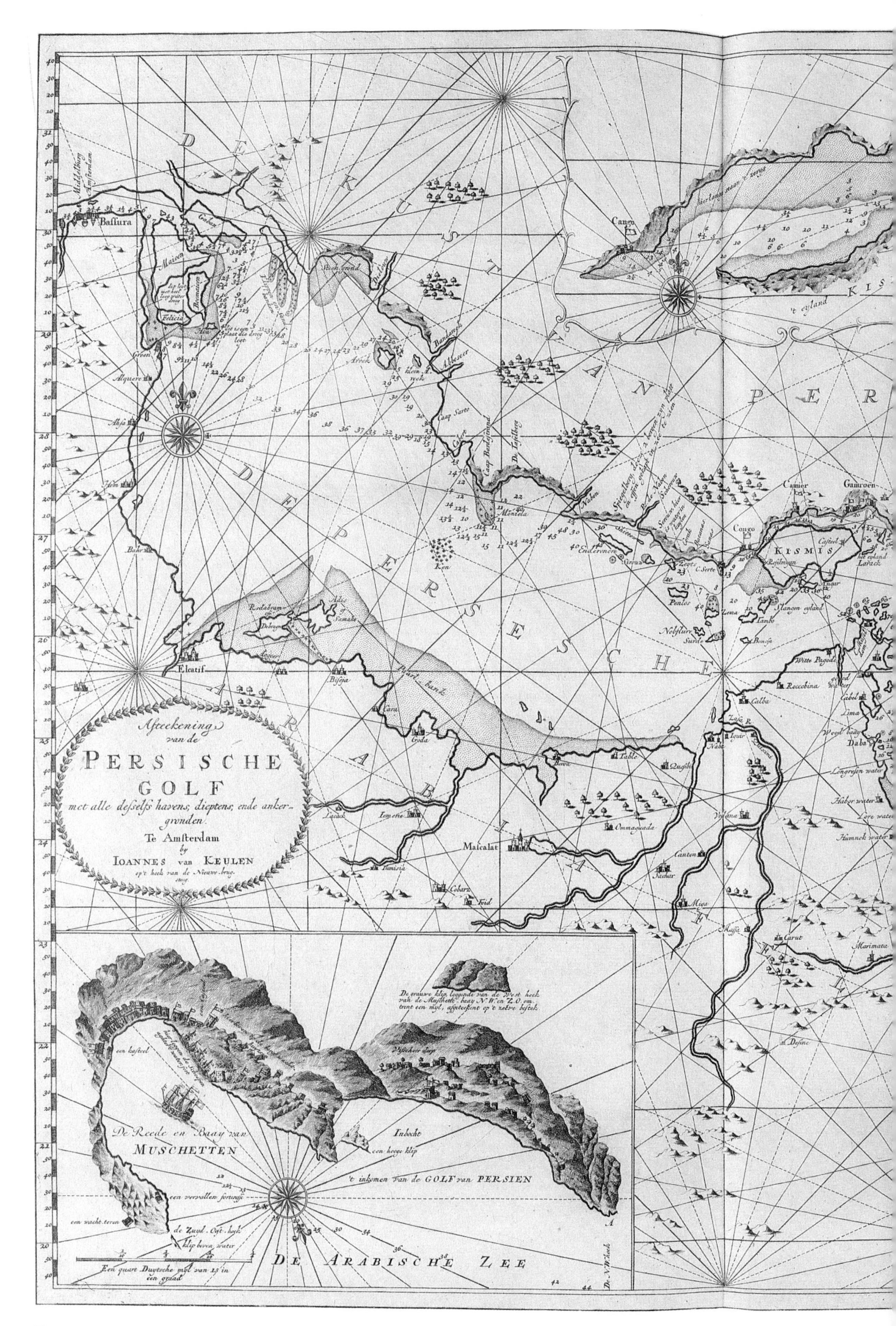
Afteekening van de
PERSISCHE GOLF
met alle deszelfs havens, dieptens, ende anker-gronden.
Te Amsterdam
by
IOANNES van KEULEN
op 't hoek van de Nieuwe-brug-steeg
De Reede en Baay van MUSCHETTEN
DE ARABISCHE ZEE
't inkomen van de GOLF van PERSIEN
Een quart Duytsche myl van 15 in een graad
een kasteel
Inbocht
een hooge klip
een vervallen fortresje
een wacht toren
de Zuyd-Oost hoek
klip boven water
Bassura
Elcatif
Mascalat
KISMIS
Congo
Camier
Gamroen
Witte Pagode
Ommagueda

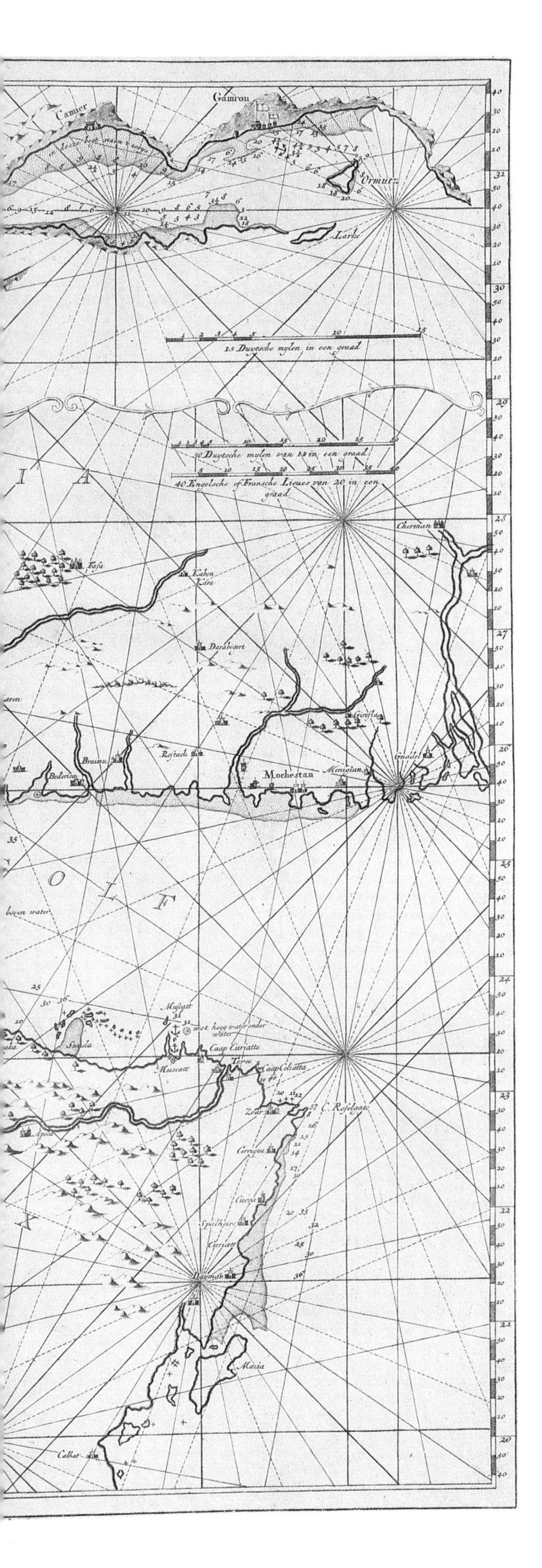

Plate 28

Van Keulen chart of the Gulf of 1753, the first map to show 'Green'.
(General State Archives of The Netherlands, Maps and Drawings Department, VEL S 6A)

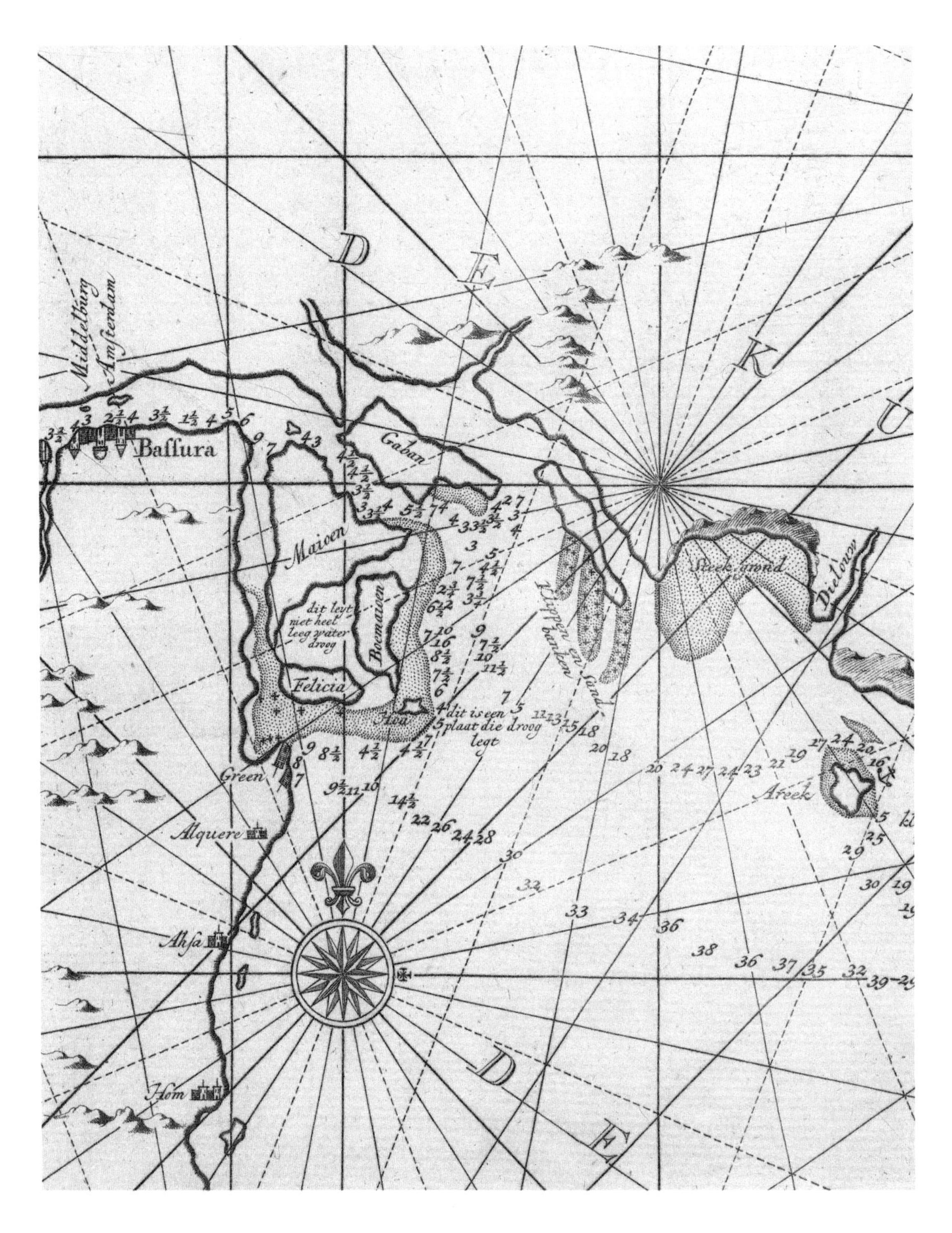

Plate 29 Detail of the chart on plate 28.

The first mention of Grain on a map

Up to 1753, there had been no detailed Dutch manual on navigation in Asia on the free market. The five-volume nautical atlas by Johannes van Keulen only covered the Atlantic and the Mediterranean. For the Indian Ocean and the Pacific (the area which was closed to Dutch shipping by the Dutch East India Company's charter unless licensed by a Company permit) there was only the English manual by Thornton. Like several other charts in his atlas, Thornton's chart of the Gulf derived from Dutch charts such as those on plate 7. The most recent data on Thornton's map are from 1666. Then, in 1753, van Keulen published his sixth volume, which was a considerable step forward in terms of Gulf cartography. Van Keulen's chart of the Gulf is not innovative in its geometric precision, but it gives four names in the Kuwait area: Grain, Faylaka, Bubiyan and Hou (Awha Island). This chart is the first in which Grain figures. Also, it contains figures of the depths off Grain, so it shows that Dutch navigation had been in that area at some date before the printing of the chart. They seem, in view of the lines of depth soundings on the map, to have come directly from Bandar Abbas. Our problem is that there is no manuscript source of van Keulen's chart available and this makes it more difficult to establish a chronology for the new data on the map, and consequently for the probable Dutch expedition to Kuwait. Whatever the date of its source may be, van Keulen's chart remains the earliest printed mention of Grain (and also of the islands Bubiyan and Awha).

Tiddo Frederik van Kniphausen, the first to write about the Utub in Grain

No portrait has been preserved of Baron Tiddo Frederik van Kniphausen. He made quite an impression on his contemporaries by his energy, education and intelligence as well as by more negative characteristics such as notorious love-affairs, arrogance and aggressiveness. His activities caused the documents to be written which are the source of our knowledge of the early history of Grain. He was the cause of Canter's flight, and he was the first to write down more detailed information on Grain and the Utub. He was also the first European ever recorded trying to do trade with Kuwait. He brought the English traveller Ives in contact with the Shaikh of Grain, and his successor as Chief Resident of the Dutch trading post established at Kharg supplied the Danish traveller Niebuhr with information. In this way Kniphausen was responsible for the data on Kuwait contained in the books by Ives and Niebuhr.

Although much has been written about the years between 1750 and 1759 when he was active in the Gulf, there is not much known of the remainder of his life. He was born in Gödens, in the Prussian province of East Frisia, not far from the Dutch border. His father is said to have been a Prussian ambassador. The only name which fits then is that of Friedrich Ernst von In und Kniphausen, who represented the King of Prussia in many capitals, also in the Netherlands. In 1747 he went into service with the Dutch East India Company, where he must have known the right people for he was appointed to jobs which, financially, were very rewarding. He was first sent to China and then in 1749 he was appointed Chief Resident in Basra. At the news of his imminent approach, his predecessor Canter fled to Grain. Under Kniphausen's management, Dutch trade in Basra expanded considerably, but in 1753 he had a conflict with the Governor of Basra, which seems to have been exacerbated by intrigues by the English East India Company's residents in Basra. Kniphausen was only able to escape from Basra after paying a considerable sum of money. He returned to Java, where he proposed plans to revive the Dutch presence in the Gulf to his superiors.[26]

During the following year, Kniphausen sailed to the Gulf with some well-armed ships. With the permission of the owner of Kharg island, the Arab ruler of Bandar Rig, he built a fortress on that very same island. He used his ships to blockade Basra until the Ottoman Governor had paid him compensation. From 1754 to 1766, Kharg was a free port under the Dutch flag. Kniphausen acted in this far outpust as if he were royalty,

[26] Kniphausen's Basra affair has been described many times in books on the history of the Gulf, but the Dutch sources on this subject have hardly ever been used for this purpose. The principal Dutch documents can be found in the archives of the Dutch East India Company, vol. 2824 (section Basra), pp. 35–49 and vol. 2843 (part Gamron), fols. 46–51. In the General State Archives of The Netherlands there are also a number of letters on the subject in the archive of the Directors of Levant Trade no. 164.

protected by his loyal guard of black African soldiers, experimenting with modern methods of pearl-diving and reading whatever an educated gentleman should read.[27] Kharg was not enough for the ambitious Kniphausen. He wanted to increase the wealth and glory of the Dutch East India Company by occupying the rich island of Bahrain. As early as 1755, he put forward a plan to the Governor General in which he showed the wealth of the island of Bahrain and its weak defences. In it he made mention of the recent history of the island. A year earlier, Shaikh Nasir, the Matarish Shaikh dominating the Persian port of Bushihr, had been able to acquire the island.

...Three years ago, Shaikh Nasir supported by some Arabs from the Utub tribe wanted to conquer Bahrain, but after a siege of a few months, without achieving anything, they managed to create a dispute among the Huwala tribe and as a result were able to buy one of the factions plus their shaikh[28] by promising a yearly contribution of 20,000 rupees. In this manner, the Huwala quarreled among themselves and left the island, and so Shaikh Nasir remained master of it...[29]

[27] Ives, *Travels*, pp. 215–216 gives interesting insights into Kniphausen's character.
[28] Shaikh Hatim of the Nasur of Tahiri in Southern Persia is meant here.
[29] General State Archives of The Netherlands, Archives of the Dutch East India Company vol. 2468, section Kharg, documents inserted behind p. 52, plan of November 5, 1755.

Kniphausen's report of 1756

In 1756, Kniphausen had been attacked by adversaries who stated that the building of the Dutch establishment on Kharg island had been a mistake. Kniphausen replied with a detailed study, written by himself and his deputy Jan van der Hulst, on the military, demographic and economic situation in the coastal areas of the Gulf. The general run of this report is that Arabs are nice people, with an aristocratic government like the Europeans; they are much better than the arrogant and unreliable Turks and Persians. As a consequence, it is far better to reside among the Arabs than among the Turks in Basra or with the Persians in Bandar Abbas. In general, the Arabs are friendly to the Dutch on Kharg, and even if they wanted to be hostile, their military force is too small to pose a threat. The Matarish domination of Bahrain is so weak that the Dutch could easily capture it.

The report contains a more exact account of the recent struggle between Huwala tribes of the Lower Gulf and tribes of the Upper Gulf over the island of Bahrain. Before 1750, Bahrain had been owned for quite some time by the Al Haram of Asalu, one of the Huwala tribes. They were ousted in 1751 by a coalition of the Arab shaikhs of Bandar Rig and Bushihr on the Persian coast. After occupying the island the two Shaikhs quarreled and:

...Because of this, the Al Haram had the opportunity to retake Bahrain and they remained in undisturbed possession of the island for over two years. In the meantime, Shaikh Nasr was able to persuade the Etoubis [Utub], a tribe of Arabs of which we will report more below, to assist him in the conquest of Bahrain. He persuaded them to support this plan with the promise that he would allow them to dive freely on the pearl-banks, without them having to pay any of the customary duties. This was of no small importance to a people who were almost all divers. Strengthened by this alliance, Shaikh Nasr left with two ships and two gallivats...[30]

For Kuwait though, the most relevant part of the report is the description of Green (Grain), on fols. 10–10v of the report:

....Leaving the Euphrates and going along the Arabian coast one encounters the small island of Feltschah (Faylaka), and opposite it, on the shore, Grien (Kuwait). Both are inhabited by an Arab tribe of which we have spoken before: the Etoubis. They are formally dependent on the shaikh of the desert although they pay him only a very small contribution.[31] They have some 300 vessels but almost all of them are small

[30] General State Archives, Aanwinsten Eerste Afdeling 1889, 23B fols. 6v–7.

[31] The shaikh of the desert is the ordinary way in which Dutch sources of that time refer to the shaikh of the Banu Khalid of Al Hasa.

10

vernement affhankelijk, en moet aan't selve Con:
tributie opbrengen.
Van de Bassorase Zeevaard, daar nu aan
de mond van den Euphraat komende, moet ge:
wag gemaakt worden valt niet veel bijsonders
te melden, De soogenaamde Galijen van den
grooten Heer durven niet ondernemen tot
aan de Mond van den Euphraat waar de selve
een weijnig breet is te koomen, Zullende als
dan sekerlijk door 't holle water uijt malkan:
deren gaan, Zij dienen derhalven behalven van
de naam tot niets als de Arme Boeren, in de
Rivier te gaan Contributies afpersen, 't welk
zij somtijds selffs niet in Staat zijn van uijt
te voeren, van de Mond der Euphraat tot Basso
'ra toe woond bij na over al Zeevarend Volk, de
welke met haare vaartuijgen de heele Golff door
Tammer tot naar Mocha vervoeren, zijn egter
alle onweerbaar, van geene snaphaanen, en soo
slegt van masten, Raas, seijlen en tuijg voor
sien dat sulks tot een teeken dient waardoor men
een Bassorase vaartuijg van verre kend, den Euf:
hraat uijt komende en de Arabische kust houd ende
vind men het Eijlandje Feltscha en daar over aan
de vaste wal Grien, bijde door eene Caste Arabiere
waar van wij te vooren gesprooken Etoubis genoemt
bewoond, deese zijn affhankelijk van den Sjeek
der woestijne aan die zij eene dog egter seer ge:
ringe Contributie opbrengen zij besitten een 300
vaartuijgen, egter bijna alle slijn, dewijl de selve

Plate 30 Folio 10 of the Kniphausen report of 1756.

haar alleen tot de Paarldûijkerij die behalven het
Visschen in de swade monsson haar enigste nee
ring is, Zij Zijn 1000 man sterk bij na alle van
Houwers, Schilden, Lantsen, maar bij na in
het geheel niet van Snaphanen versien waar
meede Zij selffs niet weeten Om te gaan.

Deese Natie is bijna altijd in verschil met den
Houlas waar van Zij Doodvijanden Zijn, omme
deese reeden soo wel als aangesien de kleijn
heid haarer vaartûijgen strekt Zig hare vaart
niet veel verder als tot op de Bahrehnse Paar
le Banken aan de eenen en de Caap verdistan
aan de andere Zijde van de golff, verscheijde dif
ferente Sjeeks regeeren over haar de welke dog
alle in tamelijcke eenigheid leeven, de voor:
naamste van de selve is Mobarek Eben
Saback, Egter terwijl de selve Arm en nog
jong is een andere Mahometh Eben Chalifa
die rijk een veel vaartûijgen is besittende wel
in soo grooten agting onder haar.

Booven Green vind men de rûine van een
vesting die voor ouds door de Portûgeesen ge:
bouwd en anders geene bewoonde plaats tot aan
Catif, t Land is een dorre woestijne, op Zee buij
ten t gesigt van de wal leggen 6 onbewoonden
Eijlandjes off platen die in als Europeese Caarten
niet te vinden;

Catif is eertijds meede door de Portûgeesen bese
ten, waar van het Casteel nog in weesen, en ta
melijk wel geconserveert is, teegenwoordig is het

Plate 31 Folio 10verso of the Kniphausen report of 1756.

because they employ them only for pearl-diving. During the bad monsoon, pearl-diving and fishing are their only occupations. They amount to 4000 men, all armed with swords, shields and lances. They have almost no firearms and are even incapable of handling them.[32] This nation is almost continually in conflict with the Huwala, who are their deadly enemies. Because of this and because of the small size of their vessels, they hardly extend their navigation beyond the Bahrain pearl-banks on one side and Cape Berdistan on the other side of the Gulf. Several different shaikhs rule them, all living in relative unity. The highest ranking shaikh is Mobarak Eben Saback [Mubarak bin Sabah], but because he is poor and still young, another, called Mahometh Eben Khalifa [Muhammad bin Khalifah], who is rich and possesses many vessels, enjoys almost equal respect among them. Beyond Grain there is the ruin of a Portuguese fortress, and there are no other inhabited places on the way down to Qatif...

This report is of quite outstanding value for our knowledge of early Kuwait. It is a contemporary and very direct source. We know from other sources that Kniphausen was personally acquainted with the Shaikh of Kuwait. Dutch ships went there: van Keulen's nautical chart shows lines of sounding which proves that Dutch ships had explored the route to Kuwait before 1753. The view of Kuwait presented in this report is that of a shipping town in an early phase of development. There is a great deal of local shipping, but the ships are still small and weaponry is primitive because the Kuwaitis had no firearms. Basically Kniphausen presented Grain and the Utub as a nascent seapower. He was not interested in the land-based side of Kuwait, despite the fact that this was very considerable as Ives's account of 1758 shows.

Kniphausen does not hide the fact that the Utub form a considerable group, the largest Arab tribal group described in his report. He gives a relatively favourable description of their political structure, which seems to be an oligarchy of heads of families in which the head of the Al-Sabah family is recognized as being the highest in rank, although in 1756 the head of the Al-Sabah was a young man, who was not very wealthy. As far as wealth and ships were concerned, the Al-Khalifa were more conspicuous. In this light it is understandable that the Al-Khalifa became the leaders of the great Kuwaiti migrations in later years.

The ruined Portuguese fortress mentioned by Kniphausen is an error. There may have been the remains of a fortress, but the Portuguese never engaged in military activities in the Kuwait area.

[32] This stands in strange contrast to the remark in the aforementioned Ottoman document of 1701. There are several possibilities. The Pasha of Basra may have exaggerated the military strength of the Utub in 1701, and Kniphausen may have wanted to show the Arabs weaker than they really were because of the political motives in his reports. If this is the case, it is still strange that Kniphausen refers to firearms being used by most other tribes.

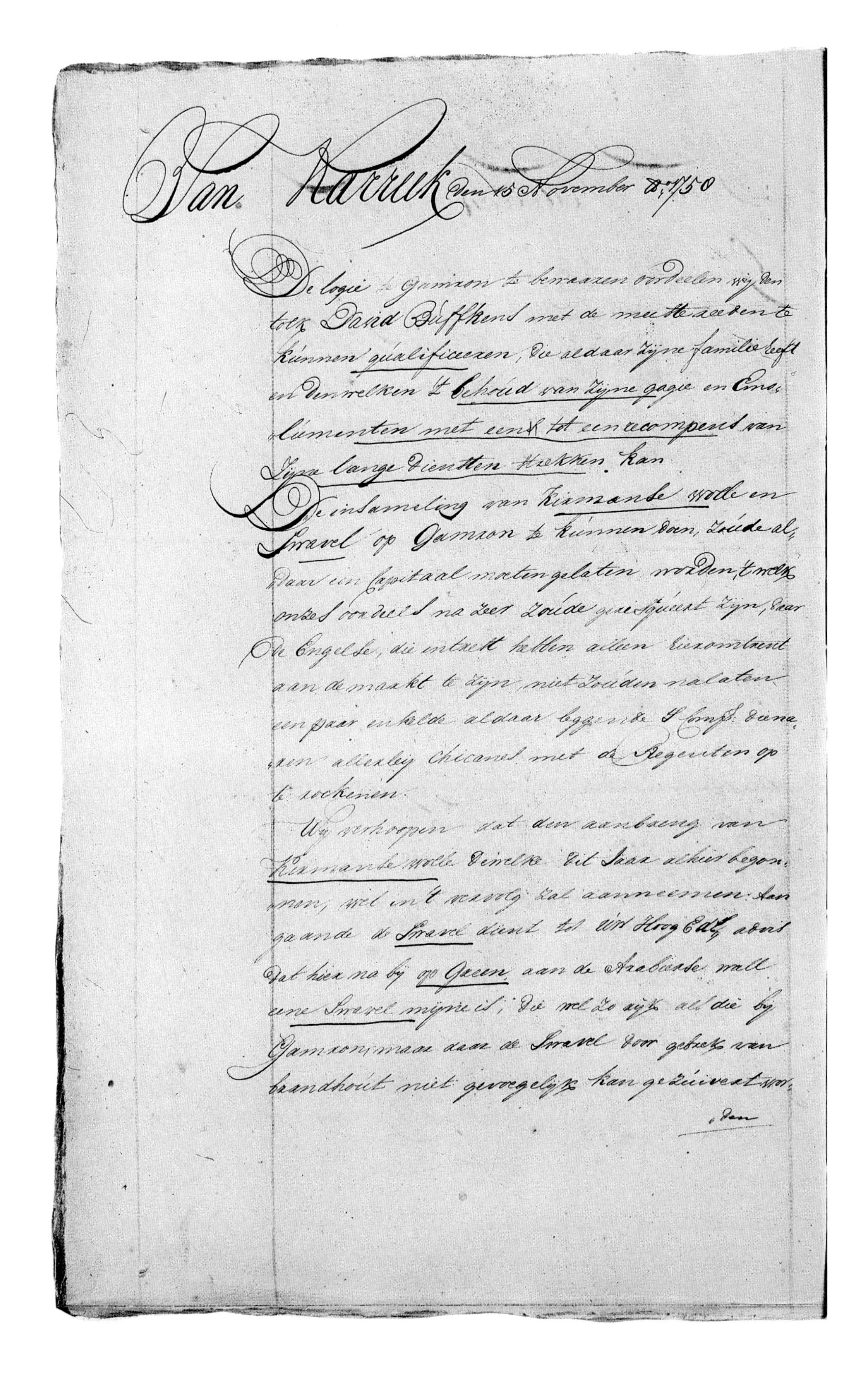

Van [illegible] den 15 November A° 1758

De logie te Gamron te bewaaren oordeelen wij den
tolk David Buffkens met de meeste reeden te
kunnen qualificeeren, die aldaar zijne familie heeft
en den welken 't behoud van zijne gagie en Emo-
lumenten met eens tot een recompens van
zijne lange diensten strekken kan.
De insameling van Kiamanse wolle en
Swavel op Gamron te kunnen doen, zoude aldaar een Capitaal moeten gelaten worden, 't welk
onzes oordeels na zee zoude [illegible] zijn, daar
de Engelse, die intrek hebben alleen hieromtrent
aan de maakt te zijn, niet zouden nalaten
een paar enkelde aldaar leggende [illegible] diena-
aan allerley Chicanes met de Regenten op
te soekenen.
Wij verhoopen dat den aanvang van
Kiamanse wolle dewelke dit Jaar alhier begon-
nen, wel in 't vervolg zal aanneemen. Aan-
gaande de Swavel dient tot UWel Hoog Edle advis
dat hier na bij op Gereen aan de Arabische wall
eene Swavel mijne is, die wel zo [illegible] als die by
Gamron maar daar de Swavel door gebrek van
brandhout niet gevoegelijk kan gezuivert worden

Plate 32 Letter by Kniphausen and his deputy Van der Hulst of November 11, 1758, containing a proposal for trade in sulphur with Grain.

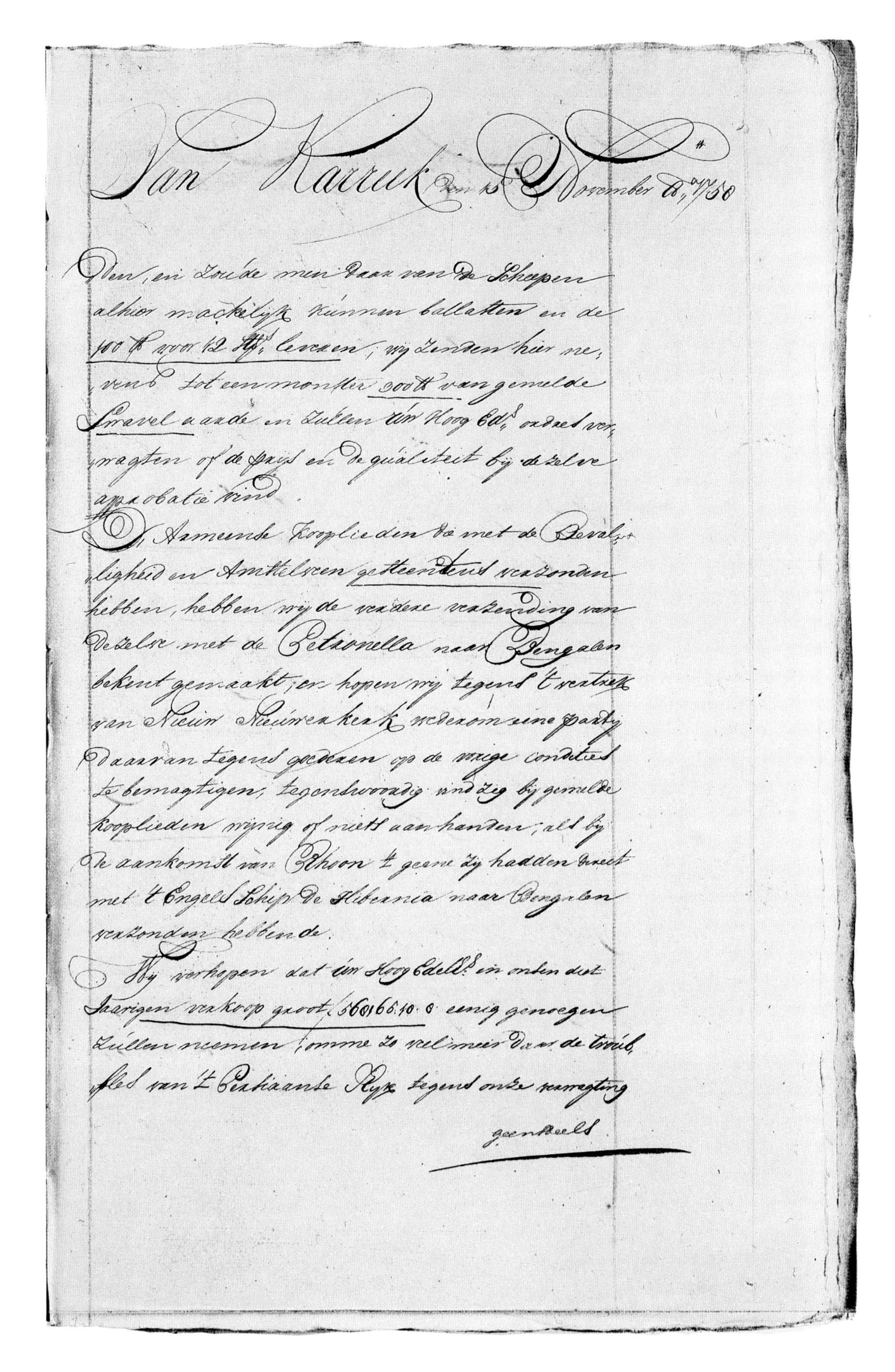
Van Karriek den 15 November A° 1750

Deen, en Zoude men daar van de Schepen
alhier makkelijk kunnen ballasten en de
100 ℔ voor 12 Stv. leveren; wij Zenden hier ne,
vens tot een monster 900 ℔ van gemelde
Gravel aarde en Zullen uw Hoog Ed. orders ver,
wagten of de prijs en de qualiteit bij deselve
approbatie vind.

De Armeense Kooplieden die met de Bevalig,
heid en Amstelveen [illegible] verzonden
hebben, hebben wij de verdere verzending van
deselve met de Petronella naar Bengalen
bekent gemaakt, en hopen wij tegens 't vertrek
van Nieuw Nieuwerkerk wederom eene party
daarvan tegens gedaane op de vorige conditie
te bemagtigen; tegenswoordig zijn bij gemelde
Kooplieden weinig of niets aan handen; als bij
de aankomst van Chason 't geene zij hadden direct
met 't Engels Schip de Hibernia naar Bengalen
verzonden hebbende.

Wij verhopen dat uw Hoog Edele in onsen dit
jaarigen verkoop groot f 568165.10.8 eenig genoegen
zullen neemen; omme zo veel meer daar de troubles
des van 't Perziaansche Rijk tegens onse verwagting
geentheels

(General State Archives of The Netherlands, Archives of the Dutch East India Company vol. 2968, pp. 10–11)

In 1758, Kniphausen made a proposal to his superiors to start trading with Grain. This proposal can be seen on plate 32, a translation of the relevant part following below:

...Concerning the sulphur, Your Honours are informed that near here in Green on the Arab coast there is a sulphur mine which is at least as rich as the one near Bandar Abbas, but in Green the sulphur cannot be refined due to a lack of firewood. The sulphur could easily be used as ballast in the ship and could be supplied at a cost of 12 stuivers[33] for one hundred pounds. We send on this occasion 300 pounds of the afore-mentioned sulphur-ore as a sample and we will await the orders of Your Honours if its quality and price do please you...

33 A stuiver is 0.05 Dutch guilder.

Ives's meeting with the Shaikh of Grain

In 1758, eight Englishmen disembarked near the Dutch fortress on Kharg. They wanted to travel on to Aleppo. One of them was Dr. Edward Ives, who wrote a book on his experiences. They met Kniphausen, who was still full of dislike for Basra, its Ottoman Governor, and probably also for the representatives of the English East India Company in Basra. When he heard about his guests' plans, he advised them to avoid Basra and to take a caravan to Aleppo by way of Grain instead. Kniphausen told the Englishmen that he knew the Shaikh of that place, who was under some obligation to him. One of the Dutch boats was sent to Grain to carry the Shaikh to Kharg for negotiations about the trip. These negotiations did not prosper. Kniphausen told his English visitors that the Shaikh thought that they were wealthy people and because of that had asked an unreasonable price. The Shaikh was a little angry with Kniphausen, complaining that the Resident took the side of the English against him, forgetting the many years of friendship they had enjoyed. This mention of the fact that the Shaikh had known Kniphausen for a long time seems to indicate that there had been no change in Kuwait for quite some time and that this unnamed Shaikh was probably the Mubarak bin Sabah mentioned in Kniphausen's report of 1756.

As the negotiations with the Shaikh had gone badly, the English received some advice from their countrymen in Basra and decided not to take the route through Grain but to travel along the traditional route.

All the pages of Ives's book containing mention of Kuwait are reproduced in the following pages. In connection with Kuwait, Ives's text is especially important for the insight it gives into the economy of caravan traffic and Kuwait's place in it. Many sources present Kuwait as a port, oriented towards the sea. Ives shows another side of Kuwait. We see that the Shaikhs of Kuwait are quite mobile individuals, travelling to Syria with their camels. The Shaikh is landbound, occupied with caravans. He needed Kniphausen's ship for transport to Kharg. This also seems to indicate that he was Mubarak Al-Sabah. The seaward side of Kuwait was, as reported in Kniphausen's report of 1756, controlled by the Al-Khalifa family.

top-mafts an end, but had difcharged their pilots." Upon the whole, he gave it as his opinion, that the two *French* veffels could not be going yet, but advifed all mafters, in proceeding up the gulph, to call at every port, where he would not fail to lodge intelligence. He concluded with faying, "that fhould any *Englifh* fhips get into *Baffora* river, they would then be fafe, as he was perfuaded, the country power would interpofe to prevent hoftilities."

1758.

We came to an anchor in the road about one o'clock in the afternoon, faluted the fort with eleven guns, and received the fame number in return. Captain *Lindefey*, Meffieurs *Doidge* and *Pye* went on fhore after dinner. The *Grab* faluted them on their putting off with nine guns, and at their landing they were received by the fecond in council, and the military officer, who introduced them to *Baron Kniphaufen*, to whom they delivered Mr. *Gee*'s letter of recommendation. The fame evening Captain *Lindefey* came on board, and gave us an account, that the *Baron* (who had given them the moft genteel and friendly reception) had in his opinion fuggefted an excellent plan for our future proceedings, having recommended it to Mr. *Doidge*, that we fhould land at *Grane* on the *Arabian* fhore, and fet out from thence over the *Great Defert* for *Aleppo*. That the *Baron* knew it to be a road frequented by people of trade; that an *European*, attended only by a fingle fervant, had fafely travelled over it, and that the journey would not take up more than 25 days. Captain *Lindefey* farther added, that fhould we approve of the fcheme, the *Baron* would immediately fend a *Felucca* with a meffenger to *Grane*, who fhould bring the *Sheick* of that place (a man greatly obliged to him, and in fome meafure under his influence) to *Karec*; with him he did not doubt, but he fhould be able to concert a plan for conveying us fafe to *Aleppo*.

The next morning, Lieutenant *James Alms*, Captain *Lindefey*, Mr. *Pigot*, and myfelf, went on fhore, and were very genteely received by the *Baron*. We were met by Meffieurs *Doidge* and *Pye*, *Mynheer Bofman* the fecond; Mr. *Robingfon*, an enfign in the *Dutch* artillery, but of *Englifh* extraction, and who fpoke our language tolerably well; *Mynheer Nicoli* the company's accomptant; *Mynheer Tilick* the furgeon; and *Mynheer Binkey*, the mafter attendant. The *Baron* prefently opened to us his plan for our future journey, and it appearing to be a route as little hazardous, as any we had yet thought of, and more expeditious (though lefs commodious) than that by *Baghdad*, we unanimoufly agreed to put ourfelves entirely under the *Baron*'s direction; who gave immediate orders for the *Felucca*'s going to *Grane* to bring the *Sheick* of that place to *Karec*.

In the evening we took a walk to the fouth end of the ifland, accompanied by Mr. *Robingfon*; and paffed through fome agreeable fields of corn, a few ears of which were then ripe, and fome gardens, where we faw cole-worts, beans, and peafe in perfection. We could not but take notice

3. alfo

Plate 33 Page 207 of Ives's *Travels*.

1758. *priſoners ought to be cut off.*" This was a ſufficient hint to the officer, who took care to ſee the bloody act perpetrated without delay. Nothing more than giving the above anſwer, could ever be proved againſt the general, though he afterwards was accuſed of being the principal actor in this horrid butchery, and was accordingly removed from his government, and impriſoned, till death ſet him free.

On *Friday* the 14th of *April*, to our great ſatisfaction, the *Felucca* returned from *Grane*, and brought the long-expected *Arab*. He behaved very complaiſantly, aſſuring us of his beſt aſſiſtance, and how ready he was to accompany us to *Aleppo*. He thought it his duty however, he ſaid, to acquaint us, that if we undertook our journey at this time, we ſhould run great riſk of being inſulted by the tribe of a powerful neighbouring *Sheick* *, who having a quarrel among themſelves, were under no ſort of regulation: that two perſons had been lately attacked by them, one of whom, well known by the *Baron*, was mortally wounded. He added, that this day was the ſeventh of the *Moon*, and by letters received from different places it appeared, that the great *Caravan* for *Aleppo* would be near *Grane* on the twentieth, when the camels from this laſt place were to join it; that if we choſe to travel in company with them, we might do it with much more ſafety and convenience, than in a ſmaller party; that the *Caravan* would be only thirty days in going from *Grane* to *Aleppo*, and would conſiſt of five thouſand camels and a thouſand men. The whole of this intelligence was of too pleaſing a nature to admit of our continuing long in ſuſpence; we unanimouſly agreed to join the *Caravan*. The *Sheick* ſeemed delighted with our determination, and adviſed us to leave *Karec* on the fifteenth, that we might get to *Grane* in proper time; aſſuring us, that he himſelf would return back to *Grane* in a day or two, to get the camels, *&c.* ready for our uſe.

The Baron, after conſulting with the *Arab*, determined that our baggage ſhould conſiſt of the following articles. One *Bengal* tent, two *Arabian* tents, 18 *Arabian* baſkets, which, one with another, holds about 24 quart bottles. They were to contain 72 bottles of *Madeira* wine, 58 of claret, 54 of *Mango* ſhrub, 15 of *Arrack*, 15 of cyder, 240 pounds of biſcuit or ruſk, 6 hams, 30 neats tongues, 27 pieces of ſhip beef, 1 cheſhire cheeſe, 32 pounds of butter, 2 ſmall jars of pickled *Sardinias*, 3 quart bottles of oil, 5 of vinegar, 2 bottles of muſtard, 2 bottles of powdered pepper, 20 pounds of powdered ſugar, 8 pounds of powdered ſugar-candy, 12 quart bottles of common ſyrup clarified with whites of eggs, 28 pounds of onions,

* The *Sheick* alluded to lives near *Grane*, and is the moſt powerful of all that live in the *Deſert*, having thirty thouſand men under his command; he receives fifty thouſand crowns out of the one hundred thouſand, which are yearly ſent to the *Arabs* from the *Grand Seignior*, for permitting the *Pilgrim-Caravans* to paſs unmoleſted.

12

Plate 34 Page 222 of Ives's *Travels*.

12 pounds of ginger-bread nuts, 30 pounds of *Gombroon* dried prunes, two *Cattees* of tea, two of powdered coffee, one canvas portmanteau, to hold our linnen and clothes, and a larger one for our bedding. As our whole party confifted of eight perfons, it was agreed that each of us (fervants excepted) fhould take with him 30 fuits of linnen, one *European* fuit of clothes, four or five pair of thin fhoes, a plain hat, an *Arabian Camaline*, troufers, *Turban* and flippers, and a *Turkifh Janizary*'s drefs. The above inventory of our baggage being fixed, and the Baron having acquainted the *Arab*, that he intended to accommodate us with two of his own horfes in our journey; the latter declared, that 30 camels would ftill be wanting to carry us, our fervants, and baggage. The Baron infifted, that a lefs number would be fufficient, and brought him down to twenty. It was then agreed between them, it would be neceffary for us to take from *Grane* an *Arab* of credit, whofe bufinefs would be to fettle all points with the commander of the *Caravan*, to prevent infults, thefts, *&c. &c.*

1758.

The Baron took me afide, and told me, by what he could learn, the price of a camel at and about *Grane*, was about thirty-five *Piaftres*, but he feared that we as travellers would be obliged to pay for the fervice only, more than the camel's original coft; but by a calculation he had made, he thought he fhould be able to agree with the *Sheick*, to provide us with camels, and all other neceffaries, for about a thoufand or eleven hundred *Piaftres* *. I took upon me to anfwer for my brother travellers, that we fhould not have the leaft objection to this fum, and defired the Baron to fettle matters with the *Arab* upon this footing.

The affair, agreeable to the *Arabian* cuftom, was negotiated between them by the mediation of a third perfon; the Baron and the *Sheick* having no immediate intercourfe with each other. A great deal of pompous folemnity fat on the face of the *Arab*, who treated this bufinefs as a matter of the utmoft confequence, and by figns upon his fingers, made a demand of two thoufand *Piaftres*. The Baron in return offered one thoufand, and the affair was thus debated by figns from the parties, and ferious whifperings from the mediator, for full half an hour; when they parted rather abruptly, the Baron being greatly difpleafed with the intended impofition of the *Arab*. He told us in the evening, that this exorbitant demand muft proceed from a report that we were exceedingly rich; that he was fure the crafty *Arab* had caft a wifhful eye upon our purfes, and that nothing but this, and the hopes he ftill entertained of our being obliged to clofe with him, prevented his acceptance of the offer, for the whole money would be clear gain to him; as we were immediately to depofit the cafh, and the camels which he was to buy with it, would fell at *Aleppo* for more than their prime coft. The *Sheick*,

* Eight hundred *piaftres* make one thoufand *rupees*, or one hundred and twenty-five pounds fterling.

after

Plate 35 Page 223 of Ives's *Travels*.

[224]

1758. after the negotiation was broken off, waited upon the *Baron*, and remonſtrated after this manner. " *You uſe me very unkindly, Sir. Pray what are* " *theſe travellers to you? I and my tribe have been in friendſhip with you for* " *a long time, and I could not have expected that you would thus have given* " *the preference to ſtrangers.*" The Baron was ſo much out of temper with him, that he returned him very little anſwer, but ordered a *Felucca* to be immediately got ready for us, that the *Arab* might think we were determined to go to *Baſſora* by water in order to join the *Caravan* there, where we were aſſured it would arrive in two days, after its leaving *Grane*. Our ſervants alſo were made to believe that we ſhould certainly proceed by water, that the *Arab*, who probably would be inquiſitive with them, might be deprived of all hope of our ever coming up to his demand. The Baron cloſed this night's converſation, with the following ſenſible obſervation. " *In* Europe *perhaps it may ſometimes be a proper maxim for people to deſire to be* " *thought rich; but in this part of the world, all ſhould endeavour to be eſteemed* " *poor, for the ſuppoſed rich man will ever be impoſed upon, and it is out of* " *his power to prevent it. Gentlemen's ſervants have alſo a peculiar vanity in* " *exaggerating the wealth of their maſters, and thereby often put them to an* " *extraordinary expence.*"

While things remained in ſuſpenſe, as to the *Arab*, we took frequent opportunities of viſiting our ſeveral friends upon the iſland, particularly Mr. and Mrs. *Boſman*, in whoſe gardens we paſſed ſome hours very agreeably, and ſmoked the *Calloon* and *Kerim Can* *, pipes which are uſed by the gentlemen here, in the ſame manner as the *Hooka* is in *Bengal*. The common people on *Karec*, like thoſe in *India*, ſmoke the *Hubble-Bubble*, which is made of a *Cocoa-nut* ſhell, and a *Bamboo* joint. In all theſe pipes the ſmoke paſſes through water before it enters the mouth, and is thereby very cool. The tobacco of *Perſia* too is of a mild kind, which being conveyed in great quantities to *India*, is there made into a paſte with ſugar, ſcented ingredients, and roſe-water, and thus ſmoking is made agreeable to perſons, who otherwiſe would diſlike it. The *Hooka* (the form of which is not inelegantly ſhewn in the annexed plate) is conſtructed upon the ſame principles as the *Calloon*, *Kerim-Can*, and *Hubble-Bubble*. It is indeed of a different ſhape from the three laſt, but will ſerve to give a competent idea of all the pipes that are uſed throughout *Aſia*.

In the evening of the 16th, Mr. *Doidge* learned from Enſign *Robingſon*, that the *Baron*, ſince the exorbitant demand of the *Arab*, had been exceedingly uneaſy, and very thoughtful upon our account. " He wiſhed (ſaid the " enſign) to have facilitated your journey; but as ſo much time has already " been loſt, and the whole ſcheme of going by *Grane* is likely to prove

* So called from a *Perſian* general of that name, who invented it, or perhaps from the word *Kerim*, which in the *Perſian* language ſignifies a horn or tube.

" abortive,

Plate 36 Page 224 of Ives's *Travels*.

" abortive, I am very ſure he would be greatly pleaſed if you ſpared
" his delicacy ſo far as to make the propoſal yourſelves of going by ſome
" other route." Mr. *Robingſon* ingenuouſly added, " that every other gentleman upon the iſland was clearly of opinion, that we ought to go by water to *Baſſora*, and he had reaſon to think the *Baron* was not to be excepted out of this number, however ſcrupulous he might be of delivering his ſentiments." He deſired however that the hints which he had given might be kept a ſecret from the *Baron*. Immediately, a ſhort conſultation was held between us on our preſent ſituation; and the ſame evening, with the general conſent of the whole party, I opened to the *Baron*, that " as ſo exorbitant a ſum had been demanded by the *Arab*, as the time of our continuance at *Grane*, before the arrival of the *Caravan*, would alſo be very uncertain, as well as diſagreeable, and as from what had paſſed, it was very probable we might ſtill be ſubjected to farther impoſition; I therefore ſubmitted to him, whether he did not think our ſailing to *Baſſora*, the moſt eligible route." The *Baron* ſeemed greatly pleaſed with the propoſal, and adopted it without any heſitation. He was ſo obliging as ſtill to inſiſt on our acceptance of the two horſes, he had intended for our uſe, and propoſed ſending them with our baggage, and one of our ſervants, in a *Trankey* to *Baſſora*; we were to follow in one of his armed *Gallivats*. This night's converſation ended, in our making him moſt hearty acknowledgments for the whole of his friendly and polite behaviour towards us; and in his giving the ſtrongeſt aſſurances of the earneſt deſire he had of contributing to our eaſe and ſatisfaction.

1758.

The next morning a boat arrived from *Baſſora*, with a letter from Mr. *Shaw*, addreſſed to Mr. *Doidge*: the following is an extract.——" I flattered
" myſelf that I ſhould have had the ſatisfaction of your company, for a
" few days at leaſt at *Baſſora*; but from the doubtful manner in which you
" wrote laſt, I know not whether I may now expect that pleaſure. I pre-
" ſume your intentions may be to proceed over the *Deſert* by the way of
" *Grane*; which doubtleſs will be more expeditious, though in my humble
" opinion not ſo ſecure, as by the way of *Baghdad*. Beſides, a *Caravan* is
" to ſet out from this laſt place in thirty-five or forty days, directly over the
" *Deſert* for *Aleppo*. It is certain alſo, that the *Deſert* is not ſafe at preſent
" without a *Caravan* or ſome proper eſcort, for yeſterday I had advices from
" *Baghdad*, that an *Engliſh* gentleman, one *Barton*, coming poſt from *Aleppo*
" to this place with a few camels, was plundered ſome days ago by the
" roving *Arabs*, who have of late in particular, greatly infeſted the *Deſert*;
" and you muſt have heard at *Bombay*, that one Captain *Ivers*, going hence
" to *Aleppo*, in *September* laſt, was in like manner plundered."

The tenor of this letter confirmed us ſtill more in the reſolution we had taken of proceeding by the way of *Baſſora*. So that on *Wedneſday* the 19th, we embarked our baggage, and the two horſes the *Baron* had given

G g us,

Plate 37 Page 225 of Ives's *Travels*.

Documents on early conflicts between the Utub and the Ka'b

Kniphausen left Kharg in 1759. He was succeeded by his deputy, Jan van der Hulst, who had been co-author of the 1756 report. During his time, two other references to the Utub and Kuwait were made in reports by Dutch residents on Kharg. All these references refer to the position of the Utub tribe as allies of the ruler of Bushir in the complicated political situation in the Gulf at that time.
The two references concern conflicts in which the powerful Banu Ka'b tribe was involved. This tribe lived on the rivers below Basra. Originally the Ka'b were considered to be Ottoman subjects.[34] In the 1750's their power grew steadily and they started to levy a toll from small shipping going to Basra. Early in 1761, their Shaikh Salman wanted to conquer Bahrain, which still belonged to the Shaikh of Bushihr. The Utub, who, after 1754, enjoyed a privileged position on Bahrain, assisted the Shaikh of Bushihr. These events seem to have been the first stage in a lasting conflict between the Utub and the Ka'b.
On June 22, 1761, Jan van der Hulst reported to his superiors on the matter:

...All is in the utmost turmoil on our side of the Gulf, and the rulers of both sides are at war with each other. Shaikh Soliman [Salman] of Hassaar [Hassar], Gaban [Qubban], Dourak [Dawraq] and the surrounding places situated on the river of Basra, has slowly prepared for war and is making schemes for the conquest of Bahrain. In February, four of his gallivats went to sea and tried to take Bahrain by surprise, but they returned, after having captured some vessels, without achieving the desired result. Next, Sa'dun, shaikh of Bushihr, prepared himself for defence with the assistance of the Etoubi-Arabs from Green and passed by Kharg in the beginning of April with a force of one large ship, three gallivats and 30 other vessels with the purpose of attacking shaikh Soliman at the Basra-river. But while they blocked one mouth of the river, four gallivats of Shaikh Soliman left by another mouth and entered the anchorage of Bushihr, put fire to two ships which were at anchor there and took some other vessels away. In the end they returned without encountering any opposition. Ali Aga, governor of Basra, wanted to make peace but he got a proud reply from Shaikh Soliman. Due to this, he has declared his support for Bushir and the Etoubis. Now everything in Basra is being prepared for war on land and water...[35]

In his report of October 1, 1762, Jan van der Hulst also mentions hostilities between the Ka'b and the Utub:

34 Perry, 'Banu Ka'b', pp. 134–136.
35 General State Archives of The Netherlands, Archives of the Dutch East India Company vol. 3027, section Kharg, pp. 4–5.

...Shaikh Soliman, ruler of the places on the mouth of the river of Basra, has started a war with Soliman Pasha, governor of Bagdad and Basra, and with the shaikh of Bushihr and with the Etoubi Arabs of Green. This we reported already to Your Honours in the letter we sent with the Dutch ship Marienbosch. This Shaikh Soliman has already been besieged by the united forces of his opponents for two months in his fortress situated about four miles north-east from the mouth of the Basra river...[36]

In 1766 the Ka'b declared themselves to be Persian subjects thus becoming a more dangerous threat than ever to the Ottoman Government of Basra.[37] From time to time, there were new outbreaks of hostilities between them and the Utub.

[36] General State Archives of The Netherlands, Archives of the Dutch East India Company vol. 3064, section Kharg, pp. 25–26

[37] Perry, 'Banu Ka'b', pp. 138–149.

Part 5
KUWAIT

After traveling through the Gulf, Carsten Niebuhr, an Ostfrisian engaged on a scientific expedition to Arabia in the service of the King of Denmark, published a book in which for the first time mentioned is made of the fact that the town of Grain is called Kuwait by the local Arabs.

Carsten Niebuhr

Carsten Niebuhr was, like Kniphausen, born in East Frisia. After having studied mathematics at German universities, he left in 1761 with four other scholars on a scientific expedition to the Arabian peninsula. Only he would survive. On his way back, he arrived on Kharg in 1765. He recorded his travel adventures in the two volumes of his *Reisen*. His other book, *Beschreibung von Arabien*, is a geographic manual.[38]

Niebuhr never visited Kuwait. As a consequence, his geographic manual—not the *Reisen*—contains the relevant material on Kuwait. His information on most coastal places of the Gulf seems to have been obtained on Kharg. Many of his references to the Arabs of the Gulf seem to have been copied literally from Kniphausen's report of 1756. He met one of Kniphausen's assistants on Kharg, the very able Buschman. Buschmen had succeeded Jan van der Hulst, and Niebuhr may have had information from him and from another Dutchman on Kharg, who had been in the Gulf since the 1730's.

Niebuhr mentions that the map he published is based on an English map. This was probably Thornton's nautical chart, which we mentioned earlier. This is a chart with reasonable-quality geometry. Niebuhr put many new names on his version. Van Keulen's chart, which mentions Grain, seems to have remained unknown to Niebuhr. In his book he mentions D'Anville's map in connection with Faylaka, but he makes no remarks about Kazima, which is also on D'Anville's map. On the other hand, he puts the name Kuwait on the map as a synonym for Grain.

Niebuhr's text on Kuwait includes some facts already mentioned by Kniphausen. He mentions the Shaikh of the Banu Khalid as overlord and the non-existent Portuguese fortress. He is not as blind as Kniphausen was for the desert side of Kuwait's economy and makes an interesting remark on the caravan traffic. His numbers are considerably higher than the numbers given in Kniphausen's report. A number of 10,000 inhabitants seems very high, and 800 ships also seems exaggerated. The remarks on the relations between the Banu Khalid and the Ottoman Empire are interesting in connection with the overlordship of the Banu Khalid over Kuwait. Niebuhr's scholarly turn of mind is shown in the way he includes the names of places in Arabic as well and his note referring to authors in antiquity.

[38] The original editions (in German) were printed in Copenhagen, the *Beschreibung* in 1772 and the *Reisen* in 1774–1776. A modern work on the Danish expedition is Thorskild Hansen, *Det Lykkelige Arabien* (Kjobenhavn 1962). A French translation was published in 1981 with the title *La Mort en Arabie*. Traveling in the Gulf is mentioned in the French translation on pp. 350–352 and 369.

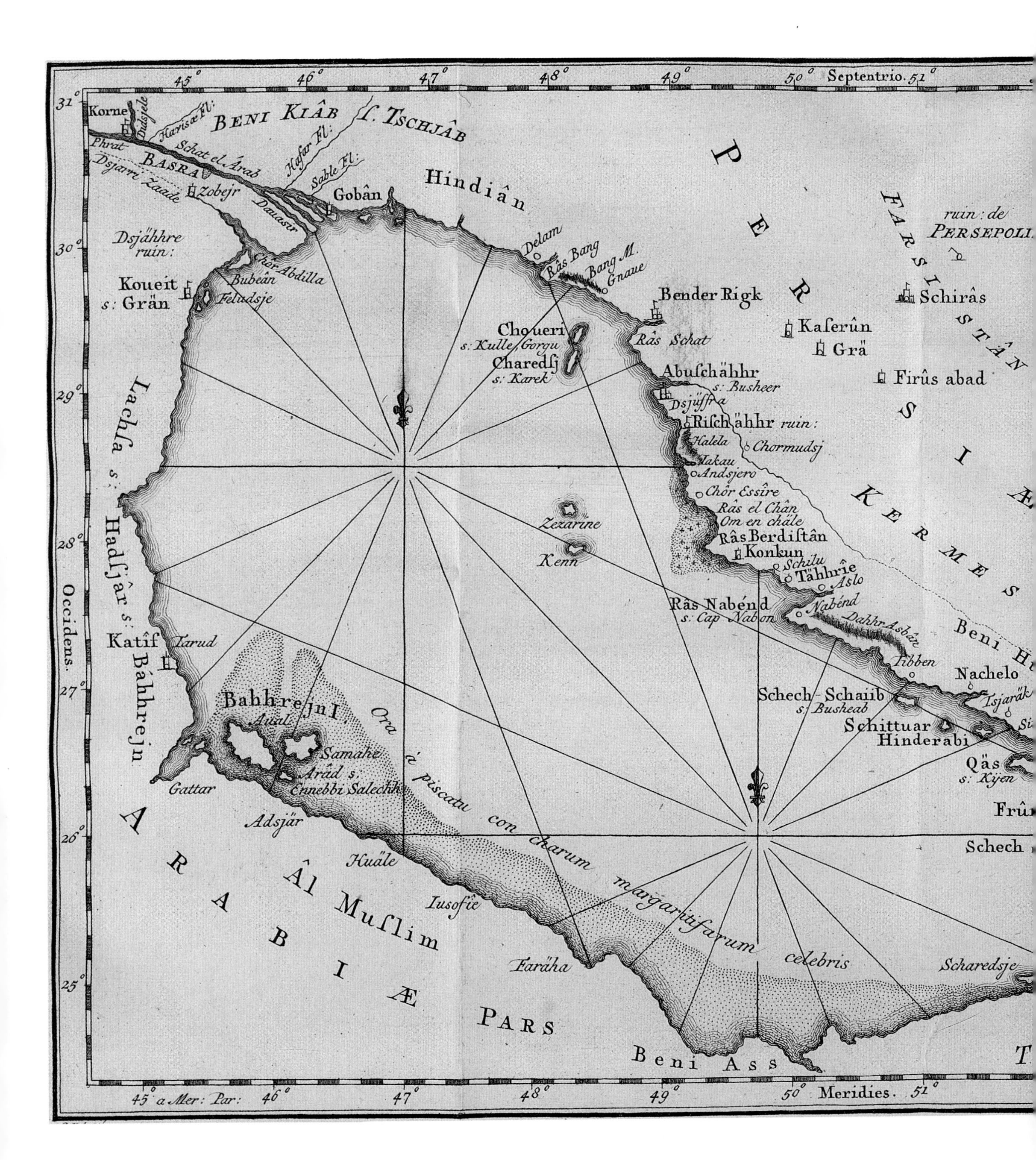
Septentrio.
Occidens.
Meridies.
45° a Mer: Par:
Korne
Dudsjele
Harisæ Fl:
BENI KIÂB
S. TSCHJÂB
Phrat
Schat el Arab
BASRA
Dsjarri Zaade
Hafar Fl:
Sable Fl:
Zobejr
Dauasir
Gobân
Hindiân
PERSIS
FARSISTÂN
ruin: de PERSEPOLI
Dsjähhre ruin:
Chôr Abdilla
Bubeân
Feludsje
Koueit s: Grän
Delam
Râs Bang
Bang M.
Gnaue
Bender Rigk
Schirâs
Kaserûn
Grä
Firûs abad
Choueri s: Kulle Gorgu
Charedsj s: Karek
Râs Schat
Abuschähhr s: Busheer
Dsjüffra
Rischähhr ruin:
Halela
Chormudsj
Hakau
Andsjero
Chôr Essîre
Râs el Chân
Om en châle
Râs Berdistân
Konkun
KERMESIR
Lachsa s: Hadsjar s:
Zezarine
Kenn
Schilu
Tähhrie
Aslo
Râs Nabénd s: Cap Nabon
Nabénd
Dahhr Asbân
Beni Hu
Katîf
Tarud
Báhhrejn
Bahhrejn I.
Aual
Samahe
Arâd s.
Ennebbi Salechh
Gattar
Adsjär
Tibben
Nachelo
Tsjaräk
Schech Schaiib s: Busheab
Schittuar
Hinderabi
Qäs s: Kijen
Frûr
Schech
Ora à piscatu con charum margaritifarum celebris
ARABIÆ PARS
Âl Muslim
Huäle
Iusofie
Faräha
Scharedsje
Beni Ass

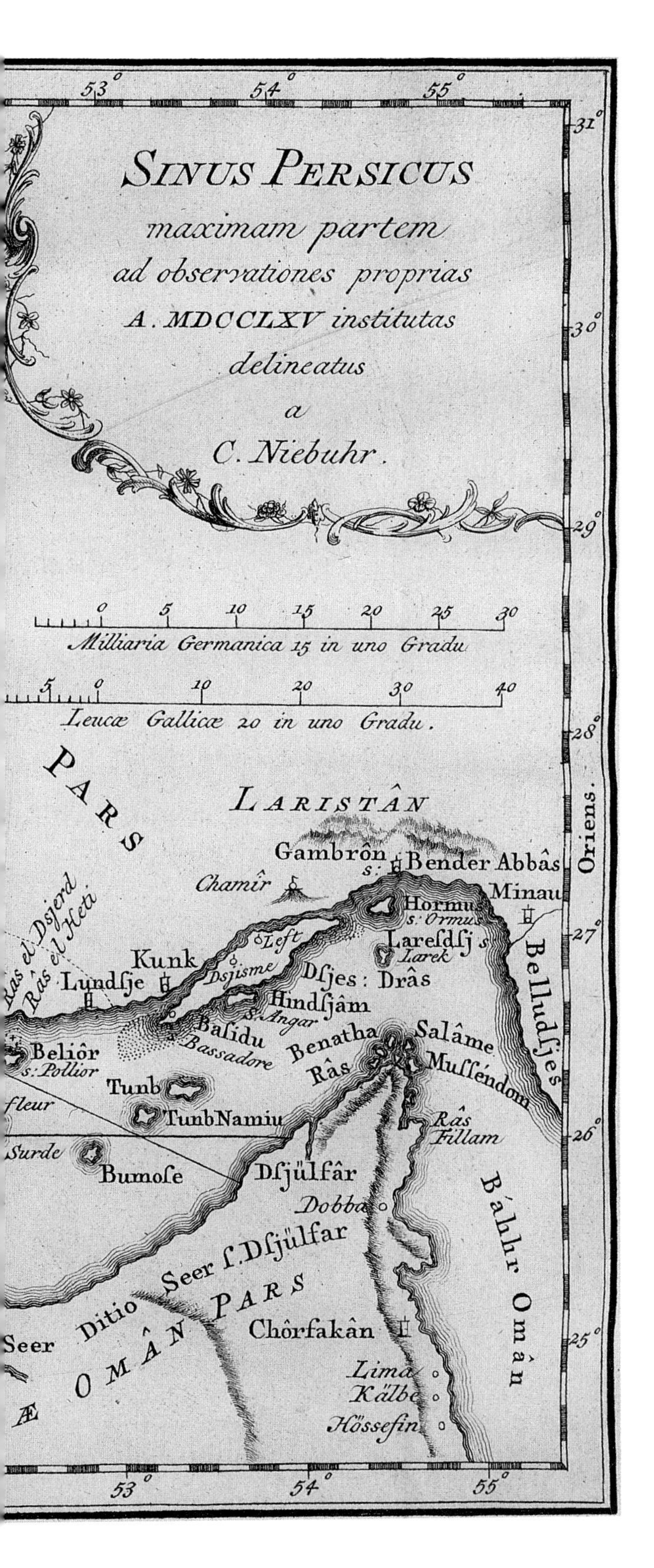

Plate 38

Map from Niebuhr's *Description of Arabia*, the earliest map to mention Kuwait by this name.

324 HET LANDSCHAP LACHSA OF HADSJAR.

De inwoners dezer ſtad betalen jaarlyks 3000 rupie voor de vrye paerlviſſery op de kuſten van Bahhrejn, aan den Schech te Abuſchähhr. De naam dezer ſtad zal hier onder weer voorkomen. Dus behoort zy veelligt niet tot het gebied van den ſtamm' Beni Chalêd.

عجير *Adsjär*, eene andere kleine haven in deze ſtreek.

كويت *Koueit*, eene ſtad en zeehaven 3 dagreizen van Zobeir of oud Báſra, en niet ver van *Chór Abdilla*, eenen langen zeeboezem ten weſten van de uitwatering van Schat el árrab. De Perſen, en in het algemeen de uitlanders, noemen deze ſtad قرين *Grän*, een naam, welke veel overeenkomſt heeft met *Gerra*, waarvan Plinius (*), en andere oude ſchryvers gewagen. Deze ſtad zou 800 ſchepen hebben. Haare inwoners genéren zig voornaamlyk met de paerlviſſerye op de kuſten van Bahhrejn, en met den visvangſt. Het getal der inwoneren rekent men gemeenlyk op 10000. Doch in het heetſte jaargety, wanneer een groot gedeelte van hun zig in de ſtreek van Bahhrejn ophoud, en veelen der overigen met kameelen voor de karavanen naar Damásk, Háleb en naar andere plaatzen reizen, rekent men het getal der inwoneren te Koueit of Grän niet boven de 3000. De alhier regérende ſtam Arabiers is van *Beni Otba*, maar evenwel den ſtamme Beni Châled te Láchſa onderworpen. Het ſchynt dat de ſtam Otba zomtyds tragt zig onafhanglyk te maken; want men zeide, dat de inwoners te Grän, wanneer de Schech van Láchſa met een leger tegen hen aanrukt, hunne zekerheid op het eiland Feludsje, welk tot hun gebied behoort, zoeken. By Grän is nog een Portugeeſch kaſteel. Den Schech te Grän behoort ook *Harar adiên*.

جهره *Dsjahbere*, eene verwoeſte ſtad eene dagreize noordwaards van Grän, legt vermoedelyk ook in zyn gebied.

Tuſſchen het gebied der Arabieren Beni Châled en het landſchap Omân woont een groote ſtam *Al Muſillim* ال مسلم, onder welken de volgende plaatzen ſtaan, als: قطر *Gattar*, حويله *Huäle*, يوسفيه *Juſofie* en فريحه *Faräha*. Een ſtam met name *Beni As* woont ook in dezen oord, hy is egter niet magtig, en zyn land is zo ſlegt, dat zyne nabuuren juiſt ook geen reden hebben het hem te benyden.

VI.

(*) In 't VI boek 32. STRABO XVI boek, bladz. 885.

Plate 39 Page from the Dutch edition of Niebuhr's book. Many of the Arab names are also printed in Arabic.

The text of Niebuhr's book

Niebuhr's book contains some interesting references to Kuwait. Although part of it is borrowed from Dutch official information (parts of Niebuhr's text are very much like Kniphausen's report), some of it is original.

...More to the North are several small uninhabited islands, and not far from the town Grän, there is a well-populated island, Feludsje [with Arab transcription], which belongs to the Arabs. D'Anville calls it Peluche.[39] Most of its inhabitants originate from Bahrain, and at present they are still mainly living from pearl-diving near that island... [p. 315 of the Dutch edition].

Niebuhr is one of the most explicit sources on the political situation of Al Hasa:

...This area was originally a colony of the Ottoman Empire, but the Arabs chased the Pasha away many years ago. Since then, only a few Turkish families have remained in the province Al Hasa, who are reputed to be descendants of the Pasha and who can still be distinguished from the Arabs by their dress. These Turks still possess large properties, but they have no part in the government. This entire area belongs to the Beni Châlêd, one of the most powerful tribes in the whole of Arabia, and it extends so far into the desert that it sometimes troubles the caravans between Baghdad and Aleppo. The actually ruling Shaikh is called Arär... [p. 323 of the Dutch edition].

Niebuhr's description of Kuwait is different in several places from Kniphausen's description five years earlier:

...Koueit is a town and harbour 3 days journey from Zobeir or old Basra and not far from Chor Abdilla, a long estuary to the west of the mouth of the Shatt al Arab. The Persians, and, in general the foreigners, call this town Grän, a name very similar to *Gerra* mentioned by Plinius (book VI, 30 and Strabo book XVI, 885). This town is reputed to own 800 ships.[40] Its inhabitants occupy themselves chiefly with pearl-diving on the Bahrain banks and with fishery. The number of its inhabitants is commonly estimated as 10.000. In the hottest season though, when a large part of them stay in the region of Bahrain and many others travel with camels for the caravans to Damascus, Aleppo and other places, the number of inhabitants of Koueit or Grän is estimated to be less than 3000. The tribe of Arabs who rule here is part of the Beni Otba but is subject to the tribe Beni Châled in

[39] See plate 24.

[40] Kniphausen's report has 300 ships which looks more probable. Maybe Niebuhr made a mistake while copying a Dutch document, writing an 8 for a 3.

Al Hasa. It seems that the Otba tribe is trying to make itself independent, because it is said that the inhabitants of Grän take refuge on the island of Feludsje which belongs to their territory. There is still a Portuguese fortress in Grän. Harar Adiên also belongs to the Shaikh of Grän.
Dsjahhere, a ruined town a day's travel to the north of Grän probably also belongs to his [the Shaikh of Grän's] territory [p.324 of the Dutch edition].

In Niebuhr's other book, the *Reisen*, there is another map showing Grain, but this time without the name of Kuwait (Tab. XLI). This map also has the island of Awha, which for the first time could be found on Van Keulen's chart of 1753.

The Persian siege of Basra 1775–1776

The mention of Kuwait becomes quite frequent in English sources after the Persian armies attacked Basra in 1775 and Kuwait became the head of the only safe passage between the Gulf and the Mediterranean.

References to Kuwait can be found in the papers of the British residents in Basra, in a diary (which survives in the Maharashtra State Archives in Bombay), and in their surviving letters in the India Office Records in London. The letters have been used by Abu Hakima for his books. The diary has remained unused by historians as yet, but gives even more specific data. It records that there was some trouble with Ottoman ships which had been sheltering in the port of Kuwait, but were handed over by the Ruler of Kuwait to the Ka'b allies of Persia. Shortly after that, the Shaikh of Kuwait, who was actually mentioned by name, went as far as sending troops in support of the Persian attack against Ottoman Basra.[41]

Abu Hakima was confused in his account of the events by the fact that he had to work with two totally contradictory sources. In 1808, a travel account of Abraham Parsons was published. This source has often been used by historians in their studies of Iraq and Kuwait. Parsons had participated in the events of 1775, but his book was only printed in 1808. It is possible that the fact that his book may have been written many years after the event accounts for its apparent inaccuracies.

What appeared in Parsons's book about Kuwait in 1808 is diametrically opposed to what was being recorded at the Basra English Factory in 1775. In his book, Parsons says that Kuwait supported the Ottomans, whereas in 1775, the English noted in their diary that Kuwait supported the Persians.[42] Abu Hakima did not altogether spot this discrepancy between Parsons and the contemporary English documents, although he painstakingly quotes from both. The discrepancy must throw serious doubt on the reliability of Parsons's book as a source.

Abu Hakima also has his doubts about Parsons, based on another remark which clashes with our historical knowledge from other, more direct sources. This remark concerns the career of Mir Muhanna, the tribal chief from Bandar Rig near Bushihr who had conquered the Dutch fortress of Kharg in 1766, and in 1769 had in turn been chased away by the inhabitants of that island. From Kharg, Mir Muhanna fled by way of Kuwait to Basra. In mentioning Kuwait, Parsons made the remark that 'Grane' was governed by a deputy of the Governor of Basra.[43] Abu Hakima makes an attempt to understand this remark, which runs contrary to the general trend of other documents, and explains that the remark is not much more than an indication of a close and friendly

41 Maharashtra State Archives, Bombay, Basra Factory Diary vol. 203 (1775) fol. 153.

42 Abu Hakima, *History of Eastern Arabia*, pp. 96–97, where Parsons's text is quoted in full.

43 Abu Hakima, *History of Eastern Arabia*, p. 85, quoting Parsons, *Travels*, pp. 193–198.

relationship between Kuwait and Basra. We are not sure whether Parsons's remark warrants this explanation. Kniphausen and Niebuhr give quite a different image of the position of Kuwait in the period 1756–1761, when Kuwait was subject to the Banu Khalid, enemies of the Ottomans. The Utub were allies of Basra against the Ka'b in 1761, only to change sides later on and cooperate with the Ka'b and Persia against the Ottoman Government of Basra—as stated in the British document quoted above. One would expect some signs of indignation in the English documents of 1775, written by the closest allies of the Ottomans, about the fact that the Shaikh of Kuwait had been helping the Persians in their war against Basra if his position was that of a deputy of Basra, but there is nothing in the British documents which could be seen as indignation. The events of 1782, when a Governor of Basra fled under the protection of the Ruler of Kuwait, are a further indication that Kuwait was not subordinate to Basra. It might very well be argued that Parsons had been mistaken with regard to the position of Kuwait, just as he had been mistaken about the attitude of Kuwait in 1775. There are strong suspicions that Parsons is an unreliable source as far as Kuwaiti policy is concerned.

From this time on, Kuwait's history could proceed along a clear track. The town prospered because of the shift of the trade route from Persian-occupied Basra to Kuwait. British ships explored the harbour for its capacity to receive European shipping.[44] In 1779, the Persian occupation of Basra ended, and borders in the area were comparatively stable for a long time. The Utub found the means for expansion far away. Reputedly in 1766, but probably some years later (there are no completely reliable sources as to the chronology of the events), Zubara on Qatar was established as the permanent abode of the Utub. In 1782, the Utub conquered the island of Bahrain from the Ruler of Bushihr. This takeover of Bahrain was the end of a long process of evolution. As maritime nomads, the Utub had been present on the banks of Bahrain in the seventeenth century, and since 1752, the Matarish rulers of Bahrain had been paying contributions to the Utub. Now in 1782, they took over the island altogether.

The Utub had become the dominating Arab group in the Upper Gulf with their own long-distance trade, a situation quite different from the one sketched in 1756 in Kniphausen's report.

[44] Abu Hakima, *Modern History of Kuwait*, pp. 28–29; *History of Eastern Arabia*, p. 100. The result of the exploration can be seen on plates 38–40 of this book.

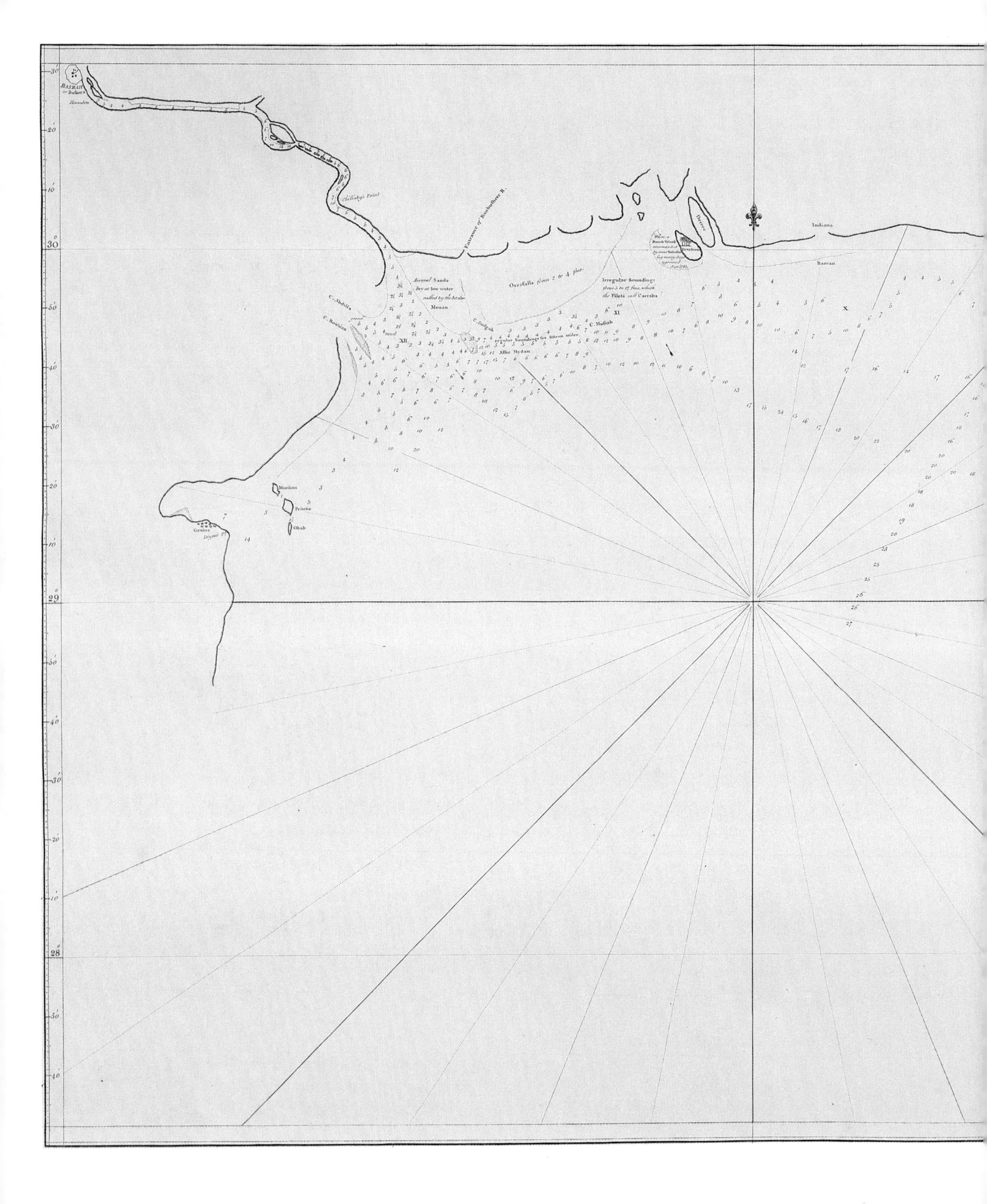

BASRAH or Bussora
Chillaby's Point
Entrance of Bamboshere R.
Indiana
Barean
Several Sands dry at low water called by the Arabs Meuan
Overfalls from 2 to 4 fms.
Irregular Soundings
C. Abdilla
C. Bouhan
C. Mufzah
Allie Mydan
Muehan
Pelzebo
Ohab

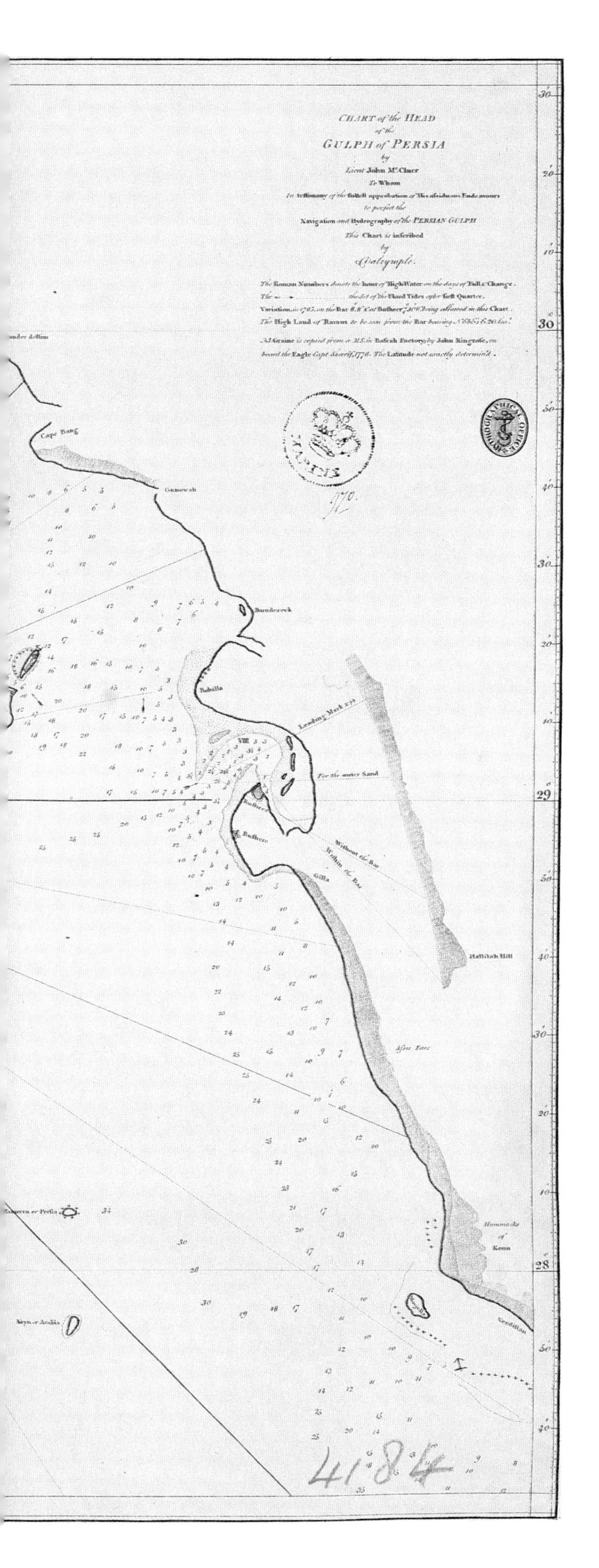

Plate 40

Nautical chart of the 'Head of the Gulf' with observations on Kuwait by the British ship *Eagle* of 1778.
(General State Archives of The Netherlands, Maps and Drawings Department, MCAL 4184)

Plate 41

Detail of the map on plate 40.

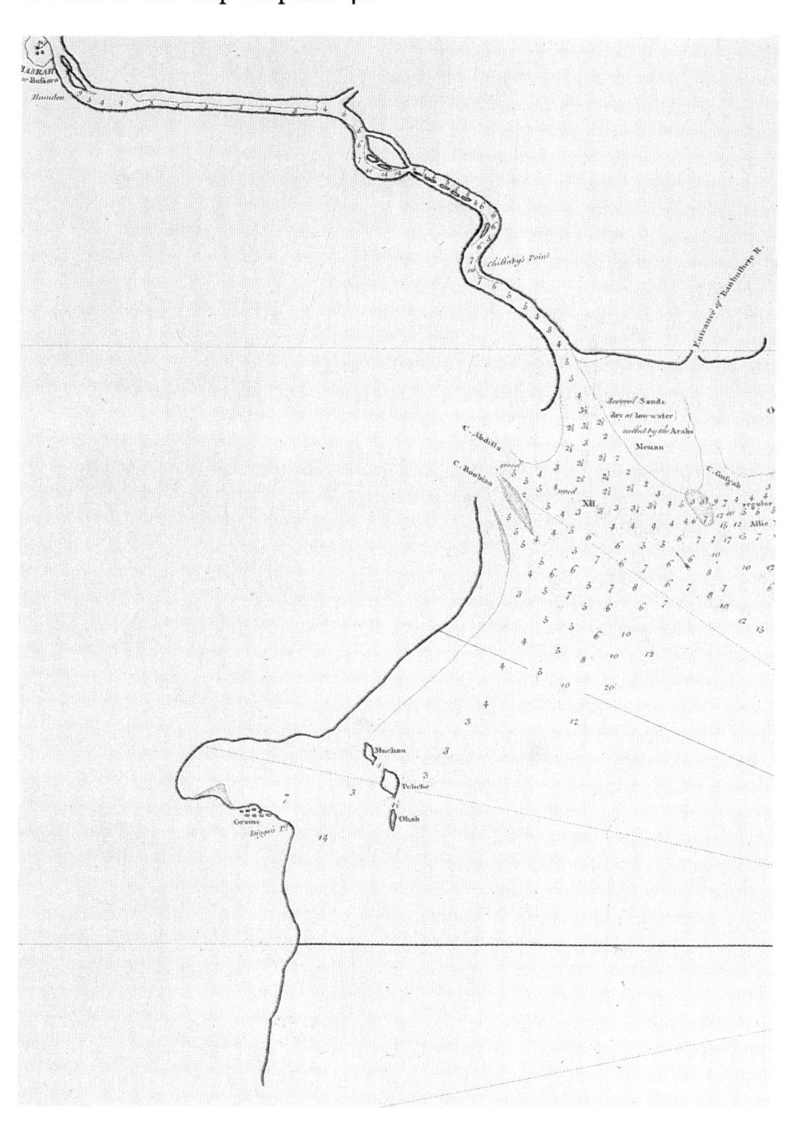

Plate 42

Laurie and Whittle's *A New Map of Arabia* of 1794 is one of the last examples of the old style of cartography. Before the modern period dawned, science was based more on respectfully borrowing from older authorities than on the scholar's own observations. This map is basically D'Anville's map (plate 24), but with additions taken from Niebuhr (plate 38). As a consequence, it gives 'Kadhema' as well as Grain. It recognizes the existence of a 'Gulf of Kadhema', but barely shows it. If this had been a map based on real observation, it would have shown 'Kadhema' in a different position relative to Grain (to the west instead of to the south). This map was made by comparing D'Anville's map with Niebuhr's map and making some scholarly guesswork.
(Collection Dr. Sultan bin Muhammad Al-Qasimi)

al Modain
Jubbel
Digel or Tigris
Babil
Varit
Kerkha
Jondi Sabur
Semauat
Tofter
Romahieh
Moke
Ahuaz
Ram Hormuz
Sura
Korn
Daurak
al Kasr
Nahr Saleh
Basian
Ragian
Baffora
Hesn Mohdi
Gebel Sinan
C. Domb
Bender Regh
Korgo
Karek
Trhah-haffar Grain
Well of Good Water
Feluche or Feludja
Bushir
el Kadhema
Gulf of Kadhema
Firuz
Andzjero
Desert of the Amer Rabaa
Plain
Well of Good Water
Zezarine
Bidehan
Kenn
C. Bard
Tangia and
Naban
Samman
C. Naban
Lar
Hormont
Tarut
Bahrain
Tibben
Nachelo
Lara
Shittwar
Congo
Hims
Khau
Andarvia
Burtion
Vakef
Merab
Ramah
Borani
Catura
Kenn or Kyen
Nobflao
Bomosa
Ahfa or Lehfa
I. Mayo
Seer
Makren
Deraieh
Salemia
Pearl Bank
Coast little Known
Mekehoan
Dhabi
Hajar
Sal
Godo
Calba
Iabrin
Salt Land
Hadram
Iemam
al Kardje
Hauthah
Mascalat
to the Hanifa and Madder
Kermireh
Soal and
Flag R.
ARAB
PERSIA
PERSIAN GULF
HEGER or BAHRAIN
ERTA

Part 6

THE LAST STEPS TOWARDS MODERN CARTOGRAPHY

In 1820, the first reasonable nautical chart of the entire Gulf was published by the London Hydrographic Office. Although it contained many improvements, it was not until 1860 that the first really good nautical chart was produced. This chart also contains the first view of a coastal area of Kuwait territory, the dark dunes of Jebel Benayeh. Finally, a geographical map of 1864 shows how, in the past century, greater accuracy could be obtained in this field, and how Kuwait was depicted in such early modern maps.

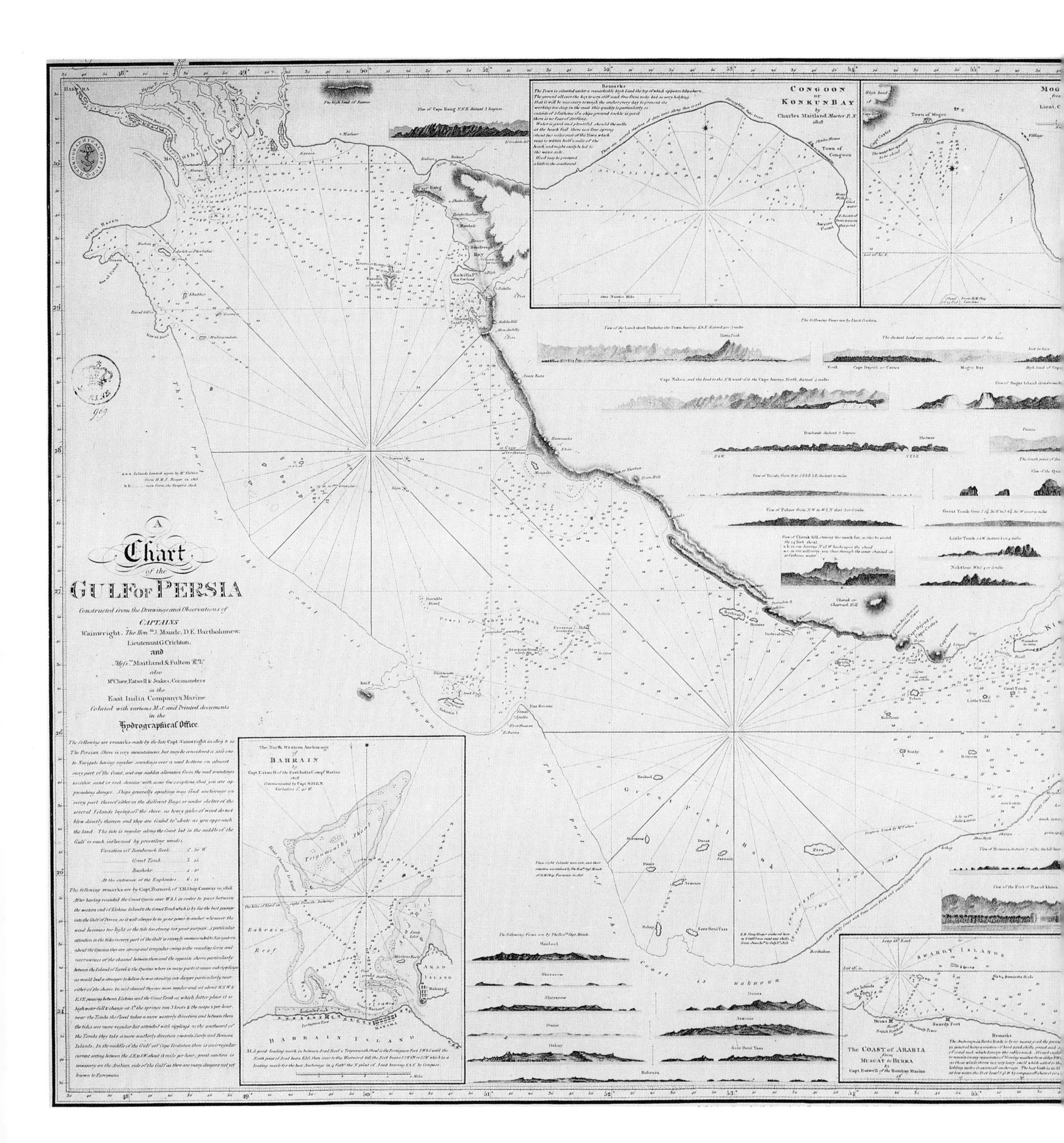
A Chart of the GULF of PERSIA
Constructed from the Drawings and Observations of
CAPTAINS
Wainwright, The Hon. J. Maude, D.E. Bartholomew,
Lieutenant G. Crichton,
and
Mess.rs Maitland & Fulton R.N.
also
M.cCluer, Eatwell & Jakes, Commanders
in the
East India Company's Marine
Colated with various M.S. and Printed documents
in the
Hydrographical Office.
CONGOON or KONKUN BAY
The North Western Anchorage of BAHRAIN
BAHRAIN ISLAND
ARAD ISLAND
SWARDY ISLANDS
The COAST of ARABIA from MUSCAT to BURKA
Pearl Bank
Great Pearl Bank

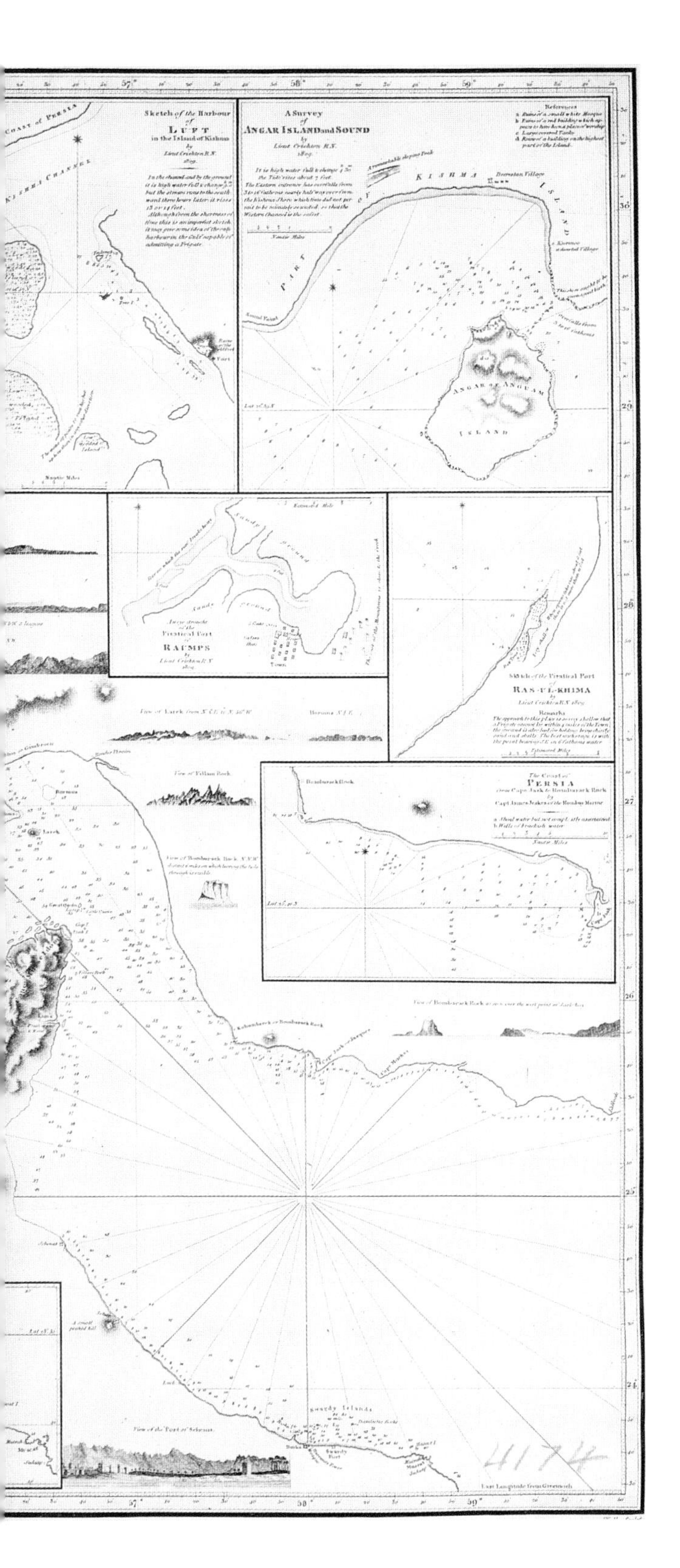

Plate 43

The British Admiralty chart of 1820 constituted a new step forward in the cartography of the Gulf, although it was not yet perfect. (General State Archives of The Netherlands, Maps and Drawings Department MCAL 4174)

Plate 44

Detail of the chart on plate 43.

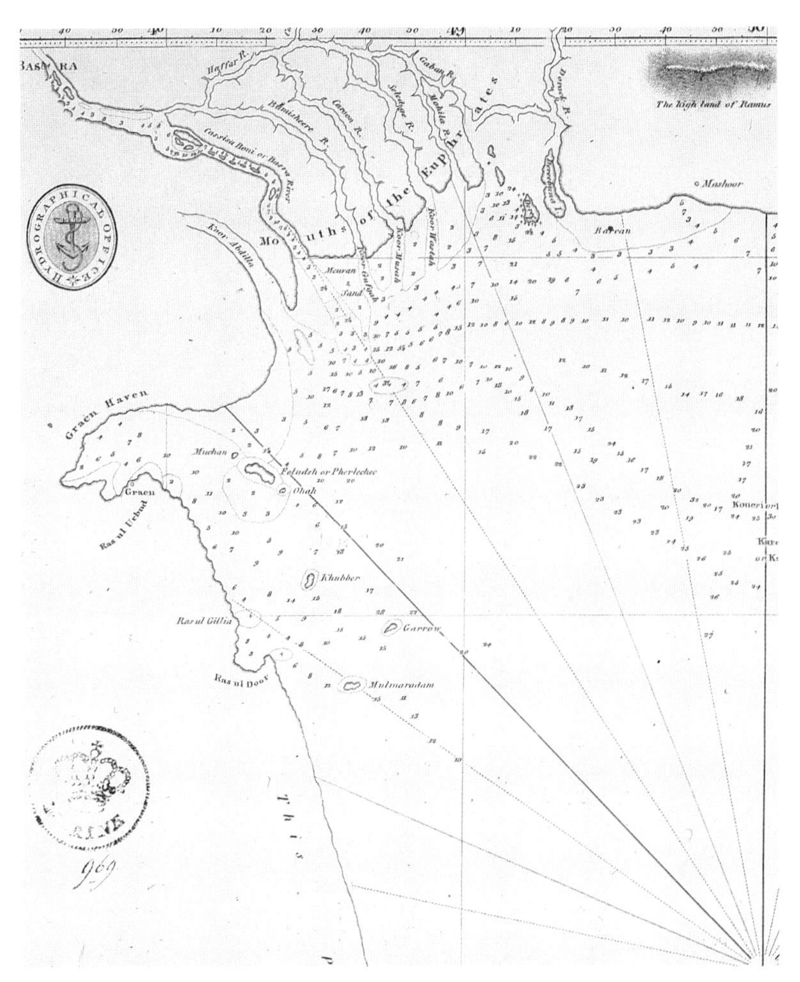

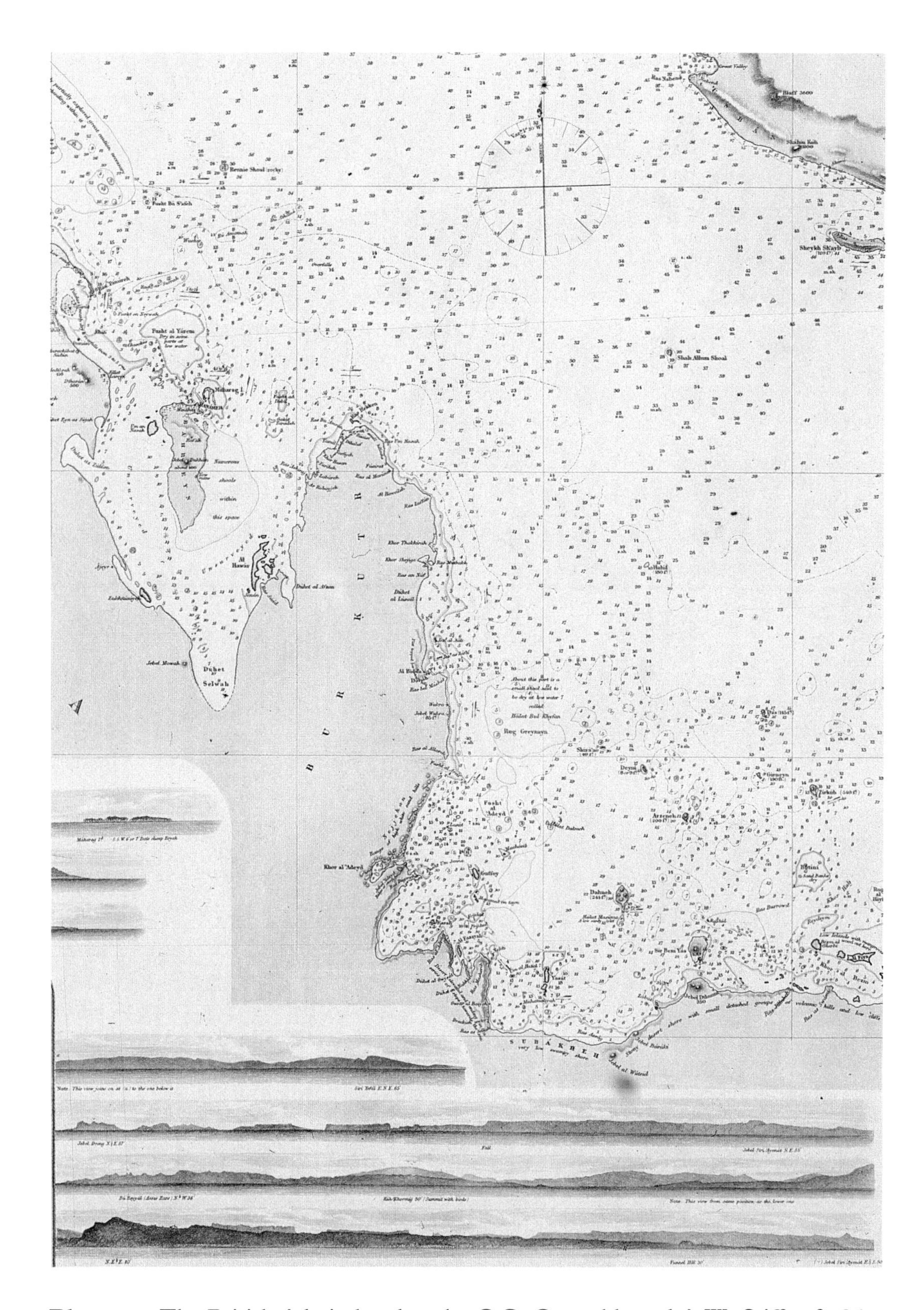

Plate 45 The British Admiralty chart by C.G. Constable and A.W. Stiffe of 1860. This is the first accurate chart of the Gulf.
(General State Archives of The Netherlands, Maps and Drawings Department MCAL 4180)

Plate 46 First picture of a Kuwaiti landscape, Djebel Benayeh in southern Kuwait. (Part of the map on plate 45)

Plate 47

Not only nautical charts but also geographical maps improved in quality in the nineteenth century. Justus Perthes's map of 1860 is a good example of German scientific cartography. Notwithstanding the closer ties of Kuwait with the Ottoman Empire of that time, Perthes still puts Kuwait outside the borders of the Ottoman province of Iraq.

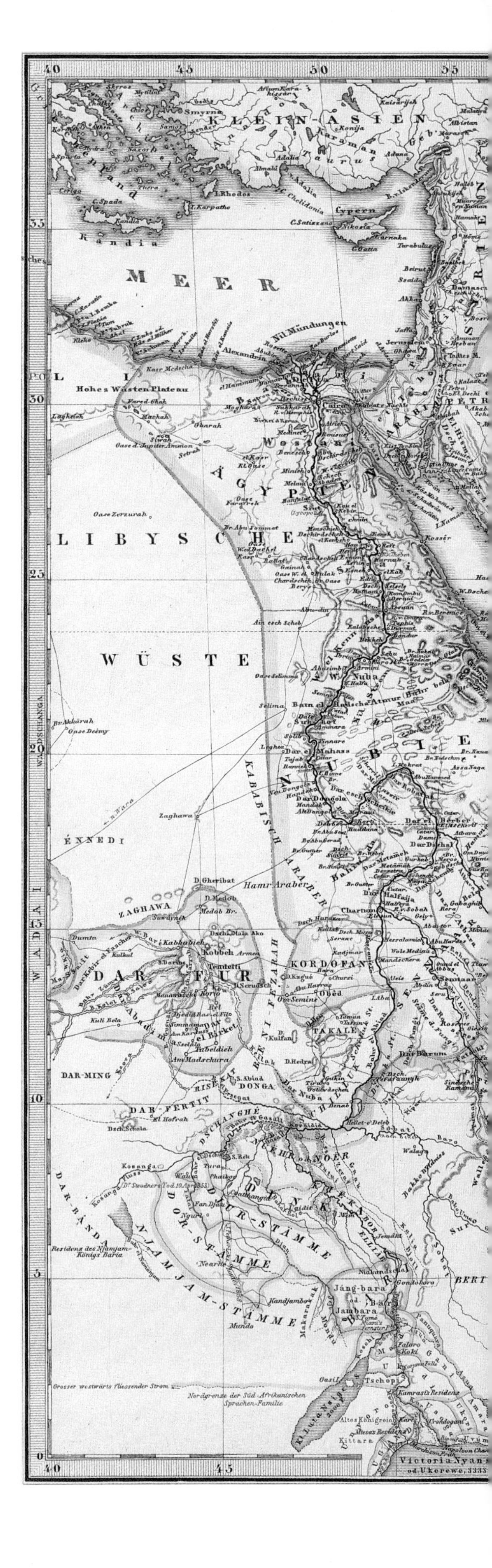

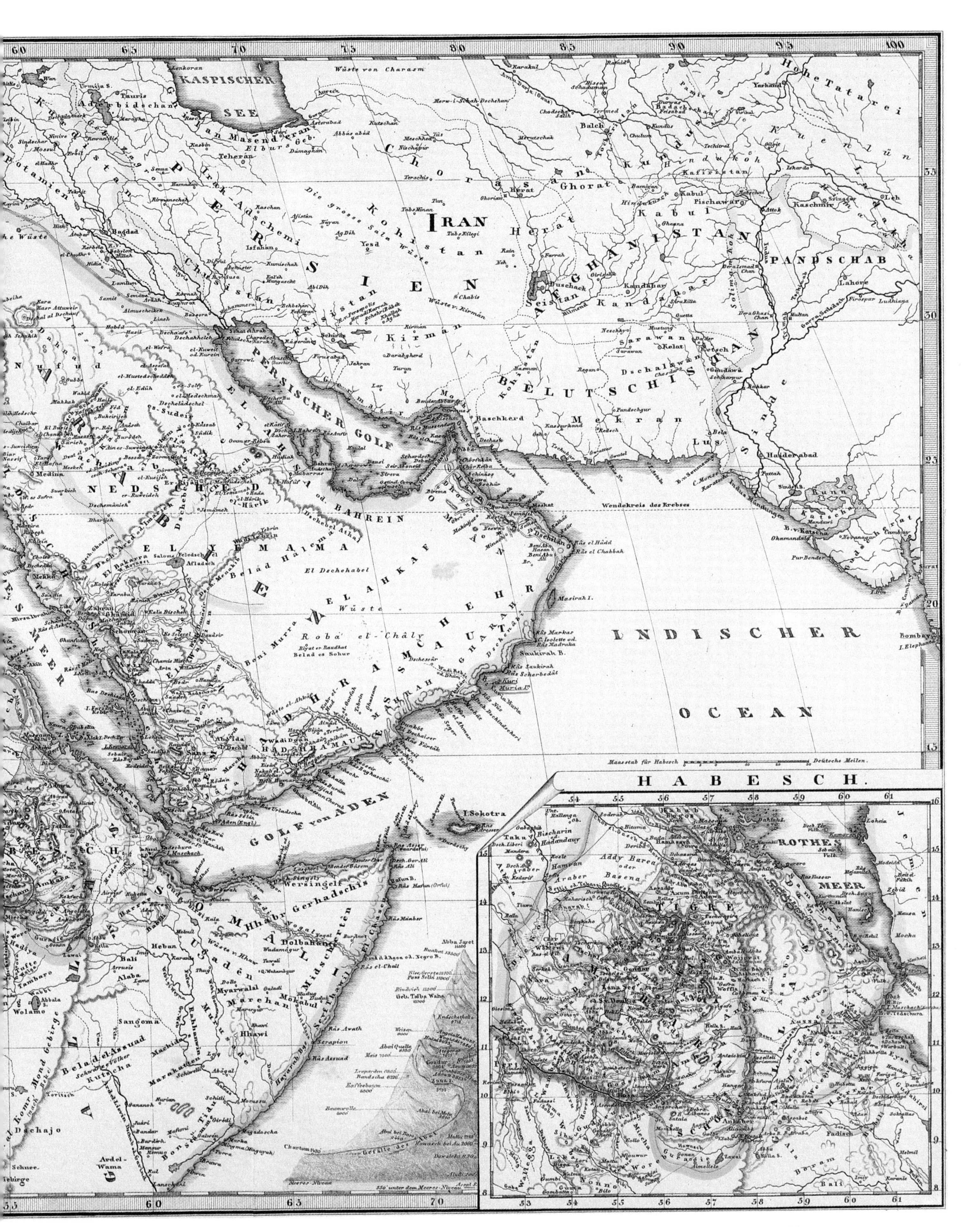
KASPISCHER SEE
IRAN
PERSIEN
AFGHANISTAN
BELUTSCHISTAN
PANDSCHAB
PERSISCHER GOLF
INDISCHER
OCEAN
GOLF von ADEN
HABESCH.
ROTHES MEER
Wendekreis des Krebses
Maasstab für Habesch
Deutsche Meilen
I. Sokotra
Bombay
Kabul
Herat
Teherān
Masirah I.

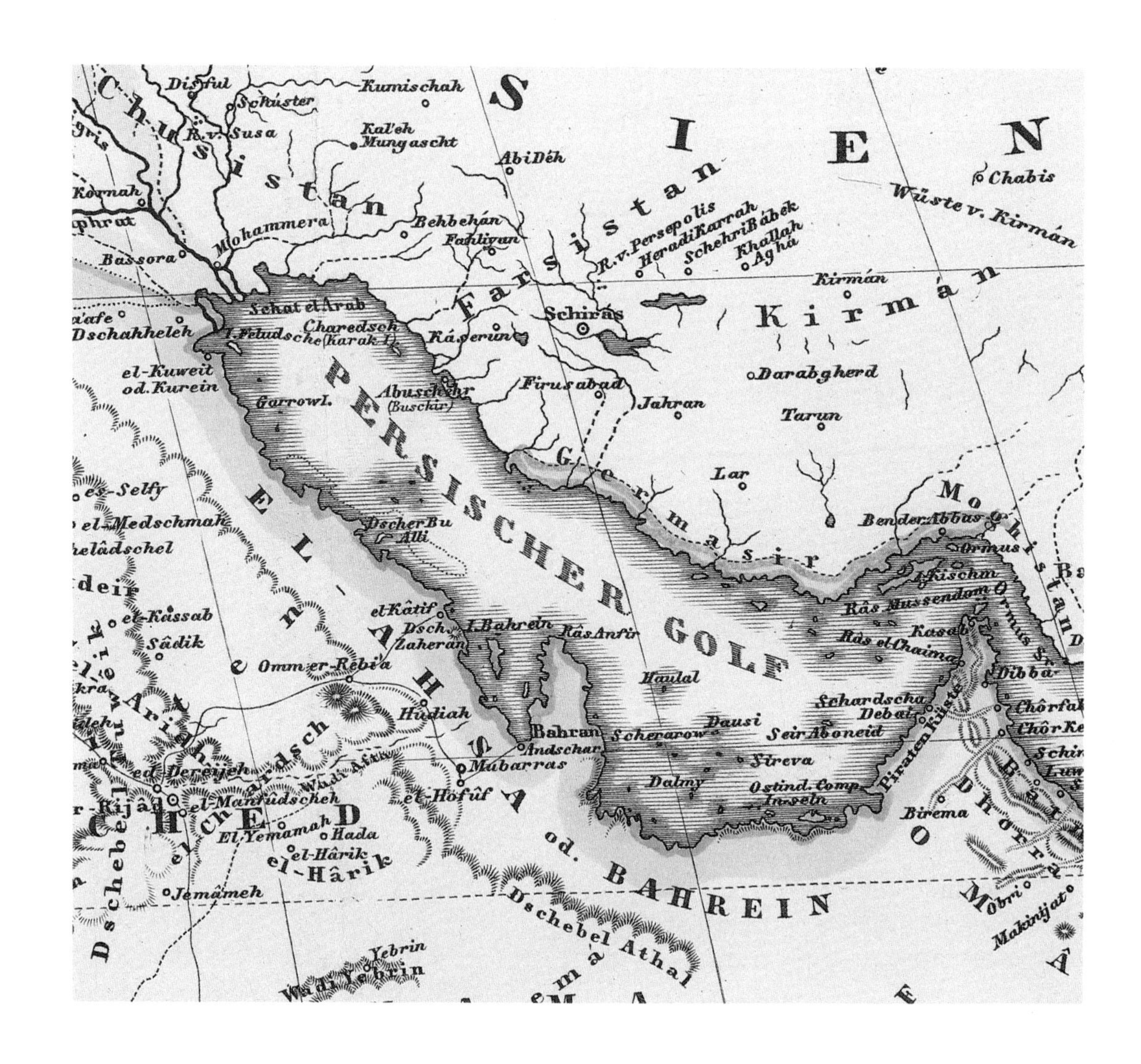

Plate 48 Detail of the map on plate 47. Kuwait has both names, Kuwait and Grain.

Conclusion

It remains uncertain as to exactly when a settlement which has lasted until the present day appeared in the territory of the State of Kuwait. Sanson's mention of Kazima indicates that this was before 1652.

The empty coast, depicted on Portuguese and Dutch nautical charts behind the Island of the Well, does not prove for certain that there really was emptiness. The crosses, which can be seen e.g. on plate no. 6 to the south of Aguada, indicate that European ships had been present off the coast; the absence of the Gulf of Kuwait on all older maps, however, indicates that no ships entered this Gulf, and Kazima deep inside the Gulf cannot be seen from the outside. It certainly existed in 1652, but we do not know its exact founding date. It was also clear to European cartographers that Kazima was outside the borders of Ottoman Iraq. The geometrical precision of borderlines on ancient maps may have been bad at times, but diagrams of the division of the Ottoman Empire into administrative districts had already circulated throughout Europe and travellers could also easily discover which place belonged to whom.

The newer generation of maps, beginning with De l'Isle's, on which Kazima is represented as a place on the coast, indicate that younger cartographers knew that Kazima was a port. Kazima's relative importance on these maps shows that it was a place of some size. These new facts appear on the maps from 1720 onwards. They may have something to do with the establishment in the area of the Utub, a seafaring tribe, which must have taken place at some date between 1701 (reference to the Utub living as refugees in Basra) and 1750 (first reference to Grain).

By the time they arrived in the Kuwait area, the Utub had travelled almost full circle around the Upper Gulf. They had started out from the desert, after which they separated from the Anaza. They then moved, probably under the rule of the Banu Khaled, towards the coast of Qatar, but were chased away from there by the Huwala. Their next move was to the country of the Khalifat, and then to Basra.

From there, they somehow arrived in the territory of present-day Kuwait. One much later source has 1716 as the year of their arrival, but nothing is certain there. In 1740, they participated—probably from Kuwait—in a general Arab move against Nadir Shah of Persia. In 1750, when Frans Canter fled to 'the village of Grain' caravans with precious loads sometimes travelled between Syria and Grain instead of between Syria and Basra. Grain's prosperity, as described by Kniphausen, Ives and Niebuhr in the years between 1756 and 1761, was based on two elements: the alternative caravan road to Syria and pearl-diving.

The increased importance of Grain or Kuwait (the latter name occurs for the first time in 1761) is due to the use of its port as an alternative for Basra. This does not mean that Kuwait was very open to foreign trade and shipping. In Basra, and in the other ports of the Ottoman Empire, European traders had a specially favoured status in virtue of the privileges (capitulations) granted by the Ottoman Sultan to the European powers. From the time of their first contact with Europeans until the early part of the present century, the Rulers of Kuwait tried to keep foreign interest out as much as possible, even though they were under a great deal of European pressure. The main reason for the existence of Kuwait at that particular location was that traders could find a safe harbour there with good connections with the Mediterranean basin, outside the influence of the badly-functioning Ottoman Government of Basra.

Bibliography

A. Aba Hussain, 'A Study of the History of Utoob', *Al Watheeka* 1 (1982), pp. 25–42; Arab version on pp. 94–107.
A.M. Abu Hakima, *The Modern History of Kuwait 1750–1965*. N.p. 1982.
A.M. Abu Hakima, *History of Eastern Arabia 1750–1800, the Rise and Development of Bahrain and Kuwait*. Beirut 1965.
Gasparo Balbi, *Viaggi* (ed. O. Pinto). Rome 1964.
Barthélémy Carré, *Travels*. London 1947–1948 (Hakluyt Society, 2nd series, vols. 95–97).
W.Ph. Coolhaas, *Generale Missiven van Gouverneurs-Generaal en Raden aan Heren XVII der Vereenigde Oostindische Compagnie*, vol. 7.The Hague 1979 (Rijksgeschiedkundige Publicatiën, Grote Serie 164).
L. Cordeiro, *Dois Capitães da India*. Lisbon 1898.
A. Cortesão, *Portugalliae Monumenta Cartographica*. Lisbon 1960.
Thorskild Hansen, *La mort en Arabie, une expédition danoise 1761–1767*. Lausanne 1981.
A. Hotz, 'Cornelis Cornelisz. Roobackers' scheepsjournaal Gamron-Basra (1645)', *Tijdschrift van het Koninklijk Nederlandsch Aardrijkskundig Genootschap*, 2nd series, vol. 24 (1907), pp. 289–405.
Edward Ives, *A Voyage from England to India*. London 1773.
Johannes van Keulen, *Nieuwe groote lichtende Zeefakkel*, vol. 6. Amsterdam 1753.
C. Koeman, *Atlantes Neerlandici*, 6 vols. Amsterdam 1967–1985.
P.C.J. van der Kroft, *Advertenties voor kaarten, atlassen, globes e.d. in Amsterdamse kranten 1621–1811*. Utrecht 1985.
S.H. Longrigg, *Four Centuries of Modern Iraq*. Oxford 1925.
Carsten Niebuhr, *Beschrijving van Arabië*. Amsterdam–Utrecht 1774 (the first edition was printed in Denmark in 1772).
Carsten Niebuhr, *Reizen*. Amsterdam-Utrecht 1776–1780 (the first edition was printed in Denmark in 1774–1776).
Jean Otter *Voyage en Turquie et en Perse*. Paris 1742.
Abraham Parsons *Travels in Asia and Africa*. London 1808.
J.R. Perry, 'The Banu Ka'b, An Amphibious Brigand State in Khuzistan', *Le Monde Iranien et l'Islam* 1 (1971), pp. 131–152.
Persian Gulf Pilot Comprising the Persian Gulf and Its Approaches from Ras al Hadd, in the South-West, to Ras Muari, in the East. London 1907.
A. Teixeira da Mota, *Cartas Portuguesas antigas na Collecção De Groote Schuur*. Lisbon 1977 (Publicações do Centro de Estudos de Cartografia antiga, vol. 105).
Edward Thornton, *English Pilot*, vol. 3. London 1703.
G.R. Tibbetts, *Cartography of Arabia*. New York 1978.